"A warm and affectionate heart fr[...] us and connects us empathetical[...] yet life-changing attitude makes our own life meaningful and has the power to heal the world. I strongly encourage anyone who encounters Kongtrul Rinpoche's beautiful book to take its profound wisdom to heart."

—Yongey Mingyur Rinpoche, author of *The Joy of Living*

"Kongtrul Rinpoche delivers a series of profound explorations and expositions on one of the most important aspects of our spiritual practice—uncovering the tender warmth and affection in our hearts. This tenderness is the root source of all that is truly beneficial in the world. Rinpoche leads us through a foundational training for compassionate vision and our own liberation, with joyful diligence and an open heart."

—Sharon Salzberg, author of *Lovingkindness* and *Real Love*

"Deep, inspiring, and disarmingly simple, this book demonstrates our innate capacity for tenderness. A warm heart is the source of compassion, loving-kindness, and equanimity, even in the face of death. Thanks to the clear mind and kind heart of Dzigar Kongtrul Rinpoche, we now have a guide to cultivating this most precious quality and letting it shine out to the world."

—Jan Chozen Bays, author of *Mindful Eating*

"It is possible to cultivate true happiness in all aspects of our daily lives and to change our reality—and that of the people around us—in the process. It's all about arousing the warmth of heart that is our birthright as humans. Dzigar Kongtrul's potent instruction manual shows you how."

—Lodro Rinzler, author of *Love Hurts*

Books by Dzigar Kongtrul

Heart Advice

The Intelligent Heart

It's Up to You

Light Comes Through

Like a Diamond

Uncommon Happiness

Training in Tenderness

BUDDHIST TEACHINGS ON *TSEWA*,
THE RADICAL OPENNESS OF HEART
THAT CAN CHANGE THE WORLD

Dzigar Kongtrul

Edited by
Joseph Waxman

Foreword by
Pema Chödrön

Shambhala
Boulder 2018

Shambhala Publications, Inc.
4720 Walnut Street
Boulder, Colorado 80301
www.shambhala.com
©2018 by Dzigar Kongtrul

9 8 7 6 5 4 3 2 1

First Edition

Printed in United States of America

♾ This edition is printed on acid-free paper that meets the American National Standards Institute z39.48 Standard.
♻ This book is printed on 30% postconsumer recycled paper. For more information please visit www.shambhala.com.

Distributed in the United States by Penguin Random House LLC and in Canada by Random House of Canada Ltd

Designed by Liz Quan

LIBRARY OF CONGRESS CATALOGING-IN-PUBLICATION DATA

Names: Kongtrul, Dzigar, author.
Title: Training in tenderness: Buddhist teachings on Tsewa, the radical openness of heart that can change the world / Dzigar Kongtrul.
Description: First Edition. | Boulder: Shambhala, 2018.
Identifiers: LCCN 2017039942 | ISBN 9781611805581 (pbk.: alk. paper)
Subjects: LCSH: Compassion—Religious aspects—Buddhism. | Spiritual Life—Buddhism.
Classification: LCC BQ4360 .K67 2018 | DDC 294.3/5677—dc23
LC record available at https://lccn.loc.gov/2017039942

CONTENTS

FOREWORD

Last year, in a surprise TED talk, Pope Francis called for a "revolution of tenderness." He described tenderness as "a movement that starts from our heart and reaches the eyes, the ears, and the hands. Tenderness means to use our eyes to see the other, our ears to hear the other . . . our hands and our heart to comfort the other."

According to the Buddhist view, all living beings—not only humans, but fish, insects, and every other creature—already possess this tenderness in their own hearts. As my root teacher Chögyam Trungpa Rinpoche used to say, "All beings have the capacity for warm-hearted feelings. Everybody loves somebody or something, even if it's just tortillas." We all have an infinite source of love in our hearts and the potential to enjoy that love deeply and to spread it widely through our interconnected world.

But although we have this wonderful potential, how to tap into it is far from obvious. For this reason, we need wise and

skilled teachers to show us the way. In this area, Dzigar Kongtrul Rinpoche is one of the most highly qualified people I
know. I have studied with Rinpoche since the mid-1990s and
have benefited tremendously from his vast learning and deep
understanding of the Dharma. His ability to communicate
the Buddha's wisdom with clarity, humor, and modern-day
relevance makes his teachings ideal for our times. Most im-
portantly, he embodies the teachings on love and warmth
in his daily life, in his relationships and activities, and in his
very presence. In other words, Rinpoche practices what he
preaches.

I am hopeful that Rinpoche's new book will help many of
us get to know and make the best of our own warmth of heart.
May *Training in Tenderness* help to heal the anxiety and polar-
ization of our world, and may it contribute to Pope Francis's
revolution!

Pema Chödrön

EDITOR'S PREFACE

In June 2016, Dzigar Kongtrul Rinpoche taught his annual Modern Day Bodhisattva Seminar in Vermont. During one of the four talks, Rinpoche spoke at length on the topic of "warmth." He described this as a fundamental quality of the heart that is the basis of all our positive emotions, such as love and compassion. Although this warmth is innate in all sentient beings, we can only experience it when our heart is open to others. The more we open our heart, the more we naturally benefit others and the happier we feel. When we experience warmth, we have everything we need. But when our heart is closed, there is no solution to our discontentment and anxiety.

This was an extremely simple teaching that probably everyone present found easy to grasp. Yet, as Rinpoche continued on his spring and summer teaching tour he had a great deal more to say about it. He taught on this subject everywhere he went—California, Colorado, Virginia, France, Spain,

Ireland—explaining it to diverse audiences from many angles. Along the way, he used various other words for warmth, including *tenderness* and, most frequently, the Tibetan word *tsewa*. Whatever the title or theme of the program, Rinpoche spoke on this topic and explained how it is the essence of all of the Buddha's teachings.

I attended four of these programs and witnessed the inspiring effect they had on each audience. But Rinpoche always urges his students to go much deeper than their initial inspiration. He encourages us to match the Buddha's teachings to our own experience so that theory and practice come together like a handshake. This process is one of the great joys and challenges of the Buddhist path.

In theory, tsewa is the answer to all our problems. Since we all possess this quality in our own heart, we don't need to depend on acquiring anything from the outside. When our heart is full of its innate warmth, there is no way for anger, greed, confusion, worry, or depression to take hold. But what does this really look like in our own life? In theory, we can all agree to the value of unconditional love and warmth, but our experiences and reactions continually present us with challenges and riddles. How do we apply tsewa in the midst of the complexity and pressure of our everyday existence? How do we view and approach others with tenderness—even those who arouse our disapproval or contempt? These are questions that we need to work out for ourselves, over a long time and with great perseverance.

Rinpoche has always encouraged students to "lean your openness" toward the teachings. This means having some level of trust in their wisdom and in the wisdom of their source, which is the Buddha. At the minimum, it means erring on the side of curiosity rather than skepticism. Such a basic level of trust gives us plenty of room to examine and experiment with the teachings, to test them in all situations until we feel personally convinced of their validity.

Thanks to the precious opportunity Rinpoche has given me to put together this book, I have been forced to examine these simple teachings more closely and to start figuring out how to apply them to my own complicated mind. Even though I have only scratched their surface, I can attest to their deeply transformative quality and to the benefits of continually contemplating them and attempting to put them into action. I hope this brief compilation of Rinpoche's teachings does justice to the vast, profound, and eminently practical subject of tsewa. I take responsibility for any errors that have entered these pages due to my own misunderstanding. May this book give many readers a strong, reliable foundation to connect with and explore their own innate, inexhaustible source of happiness.

Joseph Waxman

Training in
Tenderness

INTRODUCTION

If you are interested in reading this book—or any book of spiritual teachings—chances are that two things are very important to you. One is the development of your own mind and heart. You may think of yourself as on a path toward a fully awakened state, or you may simply want more happiness and peace of mind. Whatever your motivation, it is an honorable one that gives meaning to your life. Second, beyond your aspirations for yourself, you are also concerned about the world and the beings living in it. Naturally, you care more about some people than others, but in general you want things to go well for all who share this world and for the surrounding environment.

These two concerns—for self and other—are not competing; in fact, they are intertwined harmoniously. Our individual progress benefits the world and others, and our care for the world and others opens our own minds and hearts. This connection between individual spiritual growth and wider benefit is important to emphasize, especially in these times, when people across the globe are struggling with so much conflict and confusion and don't know what to do or where to turn. Humanity has made tremendous progress in the last few centuries—in science, technology, health, literacy, and many other areas. Great achievements have improved the lives of many. In some countries, the average person today lives like a king or queen compared to the average person of a few hundred years ago. But the effects of humanity's achievements have also been very limited. They haven't helped reduce conflict among human beings. They haven't curbed our tendency to exploit those who are weaker than us, such as helpless animals. They haven't discouraged us from exploiting the Earth itself, to the point where our planet now stands in a precarious situation. If we ever expected that material progress would increase harmony in the world, among people, and within our own minds, by now we must be very disappointed.

There is no simple solution to the world's problems. We can't impose an improved structure for society from the outside. We can't remedy greed, aggression, and confusion with a pill. I believe there is only one way to bring about greater harmony in society and the environment, both locally and globally. This is for individuals like ourselves to work on our own minds and hearts so we can change from within.

We all have what it takes to do this. Why? Because every one of us is born with a profound quality that is like a wish-fulfilling jewel. This quality has served us throughout our lives, and it will continue to serve us. However, we haven't scratched the surface of making the most of it. We've enjoyed some of its benefits, but we haven't learned how to apply it to all situations in our lives. We appreciate it, but we haven't fathomed its significance. We've relied on it, but we could rely on it a lot more.

What is this profound quality that we all have? It is the innate tenderness of our own heart. Every sentient being is endowed with a heart that is capable of having warm, tender feelings toward others. Even in a vicious creature like a snake, we can see evidence of this quality in its tender behavior toward its young. No one is unfortunate enough to be born without such a heart.

When it is warm with tenderness and affection toward others, our own heart can give us the most pure and profound happiness that exists and enable us to radiate that happiness to others. This potential for happiness is right here within us. It is not something on the outside for which we need to search and strive. We don't need to get several university degrees, work hard, and save up a lot of money to buy it. We don't need special opportunities or amazing luck. We only need this heart, which is right here within us, accessible at all times.

This may sound too simple—even simplistic. If happiness is so accessible, then why are so many of us unhappy? And even if we do experience periods of happiness, why is our happiness so unreliable and so difficult to maintain? The reason is that although this joyous, warm heart is part of our nature, most of the time its glow is hidden from us. The *Uttaratantra Shastra*, a classical Buddhist text that describes the ultimate, enlightened nature of all sentient beings, uses this example: Each of us is like a hungry, homeless person who doesn't realize there's an enormous treasure buried under the ground where he sleeps. The warmth of our heart is that buried treasure, but we can't enjoy it because we lack the wisdom and skillful means to recognize it, appreciate it, and harness its power.

It's not hard to identify the tender heart in our own experience. For example, if you have a pet, you often feel strong affection in its presence. Your heart is open to your adorable little dog in a simple, clean, innocent way. You want the best for your dog unconditionally. You do anything you can to cater to its needs and desires. And seeing how your dog responds to your affection, how it wags its tail when you enter the room, how it appreciates the connection that you have, gives you pure delight.

But such a pure, blissful experience doesn't usually remain consistent in relation to any individual. Especially with fellow human beings, there tends to be more confusion. Sometimes our heart is open and sometimes it is closed. If we pay attention, we can feel the contrast viscerally. Sometimes we feel more negativity toward our "loved ones" than toward anyone else. But in most of our relationships, there are periods or moments when the tenderness of our heart flows out exuberantly. We can experience it with our children, our partner or spouse, our parents, our friends, and people in our community. From time to time, we may feel it with strangers, people we see or read about in the news, or even fictional characters.

The context varies, but at its core the experience is the same: a warm connection to others; a simple, nonconceptual care for their well-being; a feeling that their joy is our joy and that their suffering is our suffering.

The word in English that captures this experience best is probably *love*. But *love* comes with many ideas and expectations, which vary from person to person. Each of us interprets the word in our own way. And the same is true for other words I've already used, such as *warmth*, *affection*, and *tenderness*. These words can help point us in the right direction, but if we aren't careful, they can also take us away from the essence of this basic, visceral experience, which goes beyond human concepts. When we run with our own version of a word, we tend to add layers and layers until the simple experience is lost.

In my mother tongue of Tibetan, we use the word *tsewa*. This is also a human concept, but for Westerners, *tsewa* has the advantage of being unfamiliar, so there is less chance of it being misinterpreted or narrowed down to a small, incomplete meaning. But even the term *tsewa*, if we use it too much, can start to outshine the actual experience. The word can start to seem more important than its meaning. Of course, in writing a book, one must use words, but please keep these caveats in mind and try not to let the true meaning of the words drift into something abstract.

I would like to make a clear case for the tremendous benefits of tsewa and the importance of keeping your heart open, both for yourself and for others. The tender, open heart of tsewa is an infinitely malleable resource. It expresses itself as kindness, compassion, vicarious joy, generosity, tolerance, mental clarity, courage, resilience, unshakeable cheerfulness, and in many other internal ways. It also manifests outwardly in our positive actions. Everything we do for the benefit of others, or for the sake of opening our own hearts, comes from this fundamental quality of tsewa. In this way, tsewa is really the source of all goodness in the world.

It may seem naïve or unrealistic, especially in these challenging modern times, to rely on something as ordinary and soft as your own tender heart. Most of the world is under the spell of the capitalist mentality, which encourages us to be cynical and look out for our self-interests first and foremost. This is even true in places like Tibet. It saddens me to see how so many people have given up on love and affection as a source of happiness and a remedy for suffering. Even people who are trying to effect positive changes in society—for example, by fighting injustice—often overlook the importance of the warm heart as the basis of all beneficial actions. This widespread lack of trust and understanding cuts so many people off from something as crucial to our well-being as oxygen.

By writing this book, I hope to encourage you to identify and come to rely on that tender, affectionate heart we are all born with. If you have become cynical or skeptical about love, I would like to help you rekindle your natural connection to tsewa, so you can reestablish whatever trust has been lost. Then I would like to pass down advice I have learned from my own Buddhist teachers on how to cultivate tsewa and allow it to flow more and more freely and exuberantly for the benefit of yourself and others. Since I believe that tsewa is the most valuable resource human beings possess, I hope to help you remove whatever impediments are keeping it hidden in darkness so you can live a life full of joy, meaning, and profound value to the world.

1

LIKE OXYGEN

We human beings are not like weeds in an untended garden that grow up and survive without any care. We depend on having affection in our lives. As soon as your mother became aware of your existence in her womb, she began pouring all her love and tenderness into you. Then, once you emerged into the world, you wouldn't have survived a day without her love. As you grew up, you continually received her warmth, or at least the warmth of some family member or loving human being. Thanks to receiving tsewa, you have become an adult capable of standing on your own two feet. Thanks to tsewa, you can now look after yourself and your family and contribute something to society. If you hadn't received so much love throughout your life, you would not feel any security or strength inside. You would not have a sound mind.

Our well-being also depends on our expressing tsewa to others. From early childhood, we have been learning to open our heart to parents, siblings, friends, and pets. If our heart had never developed the ability to feel warmth toward others, if there were no one toward whom we felt tenderness, closeness, and trust, we would now be in a state of painful isolation. Our mind would be imprisoned in a miserable state of narcissism.

Of course, the happiness and sound mind we enjoy are only relative. We can acknowledge that our mind isn't totally blissful and free from confusion, like the Buddha or the great sages of the past and present. We have a long way to go. Still, there are so many fortunate aspects to our lives and minds that we have to appreciate. And when we appreciate them, we should examine where they come from. What is their source?

By contemplating this question deeply, we will discover the indispensable role that giving and receiving tsewa has always had in our lives. We will come to see that tsewa is like oxygen. There's no question that we need oxygen to survive. Whether we breathe in oxygen is not up for debate or negotiation. If we're in a place without oxygen, or if we can't breathe, then our lives are in grave danger. Or if the amount we can take in is less than the full amount we need—perhaps because of a medical condition—our life will be a continual struggle. Just as our lungs always yearn for oxygen, our heart always yearns to be open, to give and receive tsewa. So when we shut down our hearts, whether intentionally or not, we suffer. We feel mentally and emotionally disturbed.

All sentient beings down to the tiniest insect want to be happy and free from suffering. Although we can only directly experience our own longing, we can infer this common desire by observing the behavior of others. In the same way, others can infer our own desire by observing our behavior. For all beings, this longing is continuous; we feel it day and night, week after week, month after month, year after year. But what really is this happiness we seek, other than the exuberant openness and warmth of our own heart? Without tsewa, is there any other source of happiness? Can we find happiness in physical comfort and sensory pleasures? In relationships? The perfect job? The ideal house? A bank balance with many digits? The American dream? Now I'm not saying these things have nothing to do with being happy. In the short term, they may well contribute to happiness. But they are not its ever-flowing, inexhaustible source. Accompanied by tsewa, all of these—and many other things as well—can complement our happiness. But without tsewa, each is just a shell of happiness—an empty, lifeless shell.

Human beings are endowed with a potential for a certain kind of intelligence that other species lack. What is the essence of this intelligence? Is it the mental ability to learn and do complex things? A young woman can set an intention to become a brain surgeon. She can take difficult classes in biology and organic chemistry, go to medical school, memorize every process that happens in the body, acquire more specialized training in neurology and surgery, spend years as an intern, and then eventually be able to operate on the human brain. A dog or a turtle can't do any of those things. Yet in their own way, animals are able to perform great feats of ingenuity. If you watch any of the nature shows, you'll see countless examples of animal intelligence. Animals that have never been given enough credit for their intelligence—crabs, rodents, fish, spiders—are capable of complex strategizing, judgment, communication, and problem solving. In this way, they may have more in common with human beings than we tend to think.

But animals don't appear to self-reflect. Even though, like human beings, they all want to be happy, they can't ponder the causes of happiness or trace happiness back to its source. Their actions, which are externally oriented, have no long-term conscious vision behind them. Although these beings seek happiness continuously, they have no aspirations to achieve a happiness that lasts. And they have no way of tapping into their own hearts and discovering an inexhaustible wealth of happiness within.

We human beings are blessed with all these abilities. So the question is, how well do we take advantage of them? How well do we look at cause and effect and connect the dots of our lives? How well do we distinguish what fulfills our intention to be happy from what sabotages our well-being? And if we do see that we're acting against our intentions, how do we change course? If our way of going about being happy isn't working— or is even adding to our suffering—how willing and able are we to try a different approach?

Of course, another key part of exercising our human intelligence is to confirm for ourselves the validity of the teachings we receive. Even though the Buddha and many other sages have identified the tender heart as the source of all goodness in the world, we have to ponder this matter for ourselves until we're convinced. We have to examine and reflect on our own lives and the lives of others. I can say to you that tsewa is like oxygen, but do you see this in your own experience? I would be very surprised if you or anyone else could be happy without tsewa, but I am not in your mind. It's up to you to look into this for yourself.

For example, say that today you fulfill one of your desires. Maybe you receive some recognition or a big promotion. Maybe you finally manage to get the perfect car or the perfect pair of shoes. Now check in with your heart. Does it feel open? If your heart feels tightly focused on *me, me, me*, ask yourself honestly, "Is this a happy state of mind?" If, instead, your heart still feels warm and tender toward others, ask yourself, "Is the fulfilled desire the cause of my well-being? Or is it the tsewa?"

On the other hand, let's say nothing is going especially well for you today, yet your heart is aglow with warm wishes for others. Do you feel content or discontent, fulfilled or un-fulfilled? How does your feeling compare to being tightly focused on *me, me, me*? How does the expansive feeling of being connected to others compare to the contracted feeling of hol-ing up in your small, separate self?

Contrasting these alternating experiences of open and closed heart heightens our awareness. Without this kind of investigation, we could feel uneasy all the time without really noticing. We could assume that our good external conditions *must* be making us happy, without realizing how anxious or insecure we feel inside.

We create or adopt so many stories about happiness, and we tend to believe in them despite massive evidence that proves them to be false. Another version of this happens when tsewa is flowing from our heart, but we overlook how well we feel. Without checking in, we assume that we must be lacking something because our outer conditions are less than American Dream–like. But if our heart is filled with a reliable source of well-being, what are we really missing?

Until you're able to discriminate clearly between what promotes and what disturbs your well-being, I urge you to keep observing your heart in this way. When you see for yourself what goes on in your own heart, you'll be newly empowered by your own critical intelligence. On the other hand, if you accept the teachings on tsewa too uncritically, you'll be relying overly on hearsay. It is always helpful to be open-minded about the Dharma, the teachings of the Buddha. But to swallow them without any examination will not bring the optimal results. Only direct experience and self-reflection will profoundly affect the course of your life and mind.

Having done my own research on this subject, I really see how two little birds can live very happily in a small nest or how two puppies can happily share a corner of a room. Just having that warmth in their hearts—a warmth that they both give and receive—is enough to make them happy. Of course, it's difficult to imagine most modern human beings feeling that kind of contentment in such minimal situations. Two harmoniously married people living in a tiny house with simple jobs would probably spend a lot of their time thinking, "I need this to be happy, I need that to be happy." But if they did go out and realize all their dreams, they might well discover that they had already possessed the happiness they were searching for. Maybe their quest led them to a few novel pleasures or helped make some aspect of their lives a bit smoother, but how many years of harmonious tenderness did they have to sacrifice? Whatever they have accomplished shows itself to be a mere shadow of accomplishment because it fails to bring them the joy they had hoped for. After all this time, the couple may end up reminiscing about their formerly simple life, when they had so much space to enjoy the flow of warmth in their hearts!

The kind of external happiness with which most of us are obsessed can never be sustained. If you depend on someone praising you, someone giving you a gift, someone making you into a big deal, you are investing in unsustainable happiness. If you feel elated when these things appear in your life and depressed when they're absent, that is a form of addiction. It's not that we should reject these things when they do come around, but if we hold on to them tightly, mistaking them for the source of our well-being, we are setting ourselves up for pain. So when they do come to us, it's wise to take them with a grain of salt. We should think twice before allowing ourselves to become emotionally dependent on fulfilling our external desires.

Even the happiness that people seek from religion doesn't amount to much in the absence of tsewa. Muslims, Hindus, Christians, and Buddhists are equally in need of tsewa. For all members of these groups, the experience of the tender heart is the same. For all of them, this warm heart is the source of everything positive in the world. Tsewa predates the world's religions; it is part of nature's design. There is nothing religious about keeping one's heart open and giving and receiving love. Any religion that fails to cherish and promote tsewa becomes an artificial religion, a dogmatic religion. Its purpose is something other than the welfare of beings. Fortunately, none of the major religions are like this. Islam, Hinduism, Christianity, Buddhism, and the other great religions of this world all honor and foster tsewa. Of course, in every group, there are people who miss the point of the religion. They fail to connect their religion to the universal quest for happiness and freedom from suffering. This kind of attitude, as we often see, can become anti-tsewa, sabotaging rather than promoting the warm heart that is as important to our well-being as oxygen.

However we may look different or seem to be wired differently, deep down we are all vulnerable in terms of needing tsewa. I think of the movie *Lonesome Dove*, where Tommy Lee Jones plays a character named Captain Woodrow F. Call. Though he's a cowboy and a very tough character, it's obvious how vulnerable he is on the inside. There's no reason for him to pretend to be so tough and to act as if he doesn't need love and affection. No one really believes that a person can survive without these things. Because of their culture, their background, or their upbringing, some people may act as if they're immune to their emotions, but in reality, Captain Call and every other tough guy needs love as much as a newborn baby or kitten. This kind of softness is a positive quality. It's a strength, rather than a weakness, to feel vulnerable and to embrace that vulnerability. It puts us in touch with our own heart. When we feel vulnerable, we intuitively know the importance of tsewa in our lives.

Appreciating tsewa helps us make wise choices in how we direct our intentions, and in how we invest our time and energy. Essentially, it comes down to choosing which of two primary experiences we want to set our sights on. Whichever experience we direct our intention toward will come to dominate our life. The first experience is that of being fixated on our own agendas. Continually engaged in various forms of struggle to accomplish those agendas, we become tighter and more fearful in our heart. We develop a strong sense of like and dislike, friend and foe, which in turn makes us susceptible to painful emotions and constantly poised to react on behalf of the small-minded self.

The other primary experience we could move toward is that of an open heart continually emanating good wishes on behalf of others and receiving their warmth with grace and ease. Free from strong prejudices and biases, we gain the confidence of being able to love others unconditionally. We are in harmony with the world, with other beings, and with ourselves.

The first option is the way of conventional modern life— the pursuit of external happiness, which never lasts or fulfills.

The second option is the way of the great sages—the total reliance on tsewa. In its simplest form, we can state our choice in this way: Do we want to have an open heart or a closed heart?

2

THE TENDER HEART IS A SEED

One of the most revered and studied works of Buddhist philosophy is Chandrakirti's *Introduction to the Middle Way*, composed in seventh-century India. The opening of the book is striking: though Chandrakirti is writing a rigorous treatise on the ultimate nature of reality, he begins by paying homage to tsewa, the tender heart. His homage employs three metaphors. In the beginning, he says, tsewa is a seed. In the middle, tsewa is the water that helps the seed grow. Finally, tsewa results in an abundance of ripe fruit.

We have already seen some examples of how tsewa has the generative force of a seed. In many ways, the warmth expressed to us by our mother and other loved ones has made us who we are. Not only has tsewa enabled us to survive, it has enabled the entire human race, as well as all the animal species in this world, to survive. The power of tsewa is at the heart of life's creation process. It is at the heart of Mother Nature herself.

Even a creature like the sea turtle, which is known for abandoning its eggs, apparently without a second thought, is driven by tsewa. Sea turtles travel thousands of miles to lay their eggs on a particular beach. Leaving the safety of the ocean, a mother will crawl onto the sand at night to dig a pit deep enough for up to two hundred eggs. After laying the eggs, she covers the pit, camouflages it with dry sand, and heads back to the sea. If the turtle is disturbed in this process, she will return to the sea, wait there, and then come back to the beach and try again. Though the eggs are left to hatch on their own, the mother's tremendous effort to set up the most favorable conditions for their birth is a sign of her tender heart toward her young. Tsewa can take many outward forms. Some of them may seem unfamiliar, but in essence, there is always the same quality of naturally flowing tenderness.

Tsewa is also a seed in that it serves as the basis for developing all our positive qualities, which have no limit. The Dharma stresses the importance of compassion—usually defined as the wish for others to be free from suffering and the causes of suffering. A traditional way to generate compassion is to think about a sentient being in a painful situation, such as a cow about to be slaughtered. Doing so arouses a powerful concern for the cow. The practice may make us feel responsible for doing something for cows—to rescue them or to eliminate the cause of their being slaughtered. We may become animal activists or stop eating meat. Even if there's nothing we can do about the scenario we're imagining, the concern remains in our mind. The circumstances may be too complex, involving countless factors, and we may not have the power to help. But the concern and the feeling of responsibility are there whenever we think of the cow's situation.

This kind of compassion is an important and wonderful state of mind to cultivate. The practice heightens our awareness of others and has a direct effect on our behavior. When we have spent a lot of time pondering the suffering of other beings, it becomes hard to mistreat them. We become more principled in how we act and speak, and we are less apt to follow our selfish whims blindly. Furthermore, our own suffering no longer seems as exceptional as it once did. We realize that all sentient beings are in the same boat. Some are going through much more suffering than others, but all of us are vulnerable.

But however magnificent the results of this practice, there is a higher form of compassion toward which to aspire. That is compassion fully imbued with tsewa. If a warm, tender heart is not at the core of our compassion, then our sense of responsibility can feel more like obligation. Our concern for others can turn into an unpleasant burden that weighs us down without benefiting anyone else. When our compassion doesn't come from its most natural and effective source—tsewa—it becomes artificial and overly conceptual. Even though we are thinking about the well-being of others, there is a strong sense of self: this is what *I* want, what *I* think is good and right for the situation. So much attachment to our own view leaves us little room to see things as they really are and to act in ways that are truly beneficial. Instead, we can become pessimistic, heavy-handed, and dreary.

Among the greatest examples of compassion in my life are His Holiness the Dalai Lama and my principal teachers: His Holiness Dilgo Khyentse Rinpoche, Tulku Urgyen Rinpoche, Trulshik Rinpoche, and Nyoshul Khen Rinpoche. When I look at any of these people, I don't see any dreariness. The Dalai Lama has lost his country and spent most of his life in exile. He has witnessed tremendous suffering and feels personally responsible for the welfare of many beings—not just Tibetans, but even those who might be considered his enemies. Yet he continually exudes cheer and warmth, which is felt palpably by all who come in contact with him. This is because his heart is always open, day and night, expressing and receiving tsewa.

When it arises from the seed of tsewa, compassion feels joyful, even in the face of immediate suffering. For example, if your loved one is ill or in pain, there is naturally a lot of stress and anxiety in the air. At that point, you can think, "This pain is too much for me. I'm packing my bags." You can shut your heart and leave, either by walking out the door or by emotionally distancing yourself. You can try to keep yourself ignorant of your loved one's suffering. Or you can choose to keep your heart open and let tsewa flow. In the latter case, you will have to share the stress and anxiety; you will have to make your loved one's suffering into more of a common experience for both of you. But this kind of sharing contains great joy. Sometimes our tenderness makes us feel elated. Other times it brings us heartache. But even in heartache, we can experience deep bliss—the bliss of a heart that is open, connected, and thriving in its natural element of tsewa.

Those who have acquired the taste of tsewa will always choose to let it flow rather than to shut their heart. Knowing the deep satisfaction of a warm, open heart makes us less attached to all the things that usually obsess us: our body, our wealth, our possessions, our time, our leisure, or our privilege to do something nice for ourselves such as getting a massage. It's not that we reject all the delightful things in our lives. But we find that none of them are as enjoyable, meaningful, or beneficial as simply keeping our heart open. Sometimes I ask myself this question, "Would His Holiness the Dalai Lama rather give a teaching or go to a spa and receive a shiatsu massage?" Even if his body needed the massage, I think he would choose the teaching because of how it would enable him to express his tsewa.

Parallel to compassion, the Buddhist teachings emphasize loving-kindness—the wish for others to have happiness and the causes of happiness. A traditional way of generating loving-kindness begins by looking at our own constant longing for happiness and its causes. Then we contemplate how all others have this same longing, every bit as intense as our own. When we understand that we are no different from other beings in this way, we see how unreasonable it is to care so much more about ourselves than others. We do so only out of sheer habit—ignorant habit. At that point, once we've shed some light on our habit, we turn our mind toward others, wishing them happiness as much as we wish it for ourselves. Then, in our daily lives, we try to behave in accord with this wish, by being kind with our actions, in our speech, and in our thoughts.

As with the meditation on compassion, there is great benefit in doing this kind of contemplation. But loving-kindness is also incomplete if it doesn't spring from the tender heart. Without the glow of tsewa, the wish for others' happiness can be superficial. We may only be paying lip service to loving-kindness. Or even worse, this positive mind-set may become mixed in with less wholesome elements. For example, we may express kindness toward others in order to prove to them—or to ourselves—that we are good. Or we may impose on other people our strong ideas about what is good for them, making our own opinions more important than their true needs. Such inauthentic kindness comes with a lot of expectations. Sometimes it brings benefit anyway, but when it doesn't have the hoped-for result, it can backfire. We can feel betrayed and resentful and even act out with aggression. This can make us feel despondent about our spiritual path and wonder why we're even engaged in such a futile effort.

When our loving-kindness comes from tsewa, on the other hand, we have the joy of feeling that another's happiness is our own happiness. Instead of letting ourselves get entangled in so many ideas and neurotic expectations, we rely on the simple, nonconceptual energy that flows from our warm, open heart. Sometimes our kind actions benefit the other person and sometimes they don't, but our love never turns sour because we're disappointed in the result. Nor do our wishes on someone else's behalf ever become mechanical. When our loving-kindness is fully imbued with tsewa, it is warm and sincere, like a mother's love. When a mother says, "I hope my child is happy," she is not just paying lip service to the idea.

The warm wishes contained in loving-kindness and compassion—the wishes for others to be happy and free from suffering—can take many specific forms. We can wish for the hungry to have food, the poor to have wealth, or the lonely to have companionship. Since there is no end to the needs and desires of sentient beings, there can be no end to our wishes on their behalf. But of all wishes we can make for others, what is the kindest and greatest wish of all? If we want our tsewa to have its vastest possible meaning, this question is something we need to look into. Say a mother wants to buy a toy for her child's birthday. Should she buy some lousy, glittering object that gives the child only a few minutes of pleasure and ends up in the next yard sale? Or should she find something well-made and of lasting value? If the mother truly wants the best for her child—which almost every mother does—she should look for something of high quality that gives wholesome enjoyment for a long time.

When we open our heart to its innate tenderness and direct that warmth into loving-kindness and compassion, we experience a love for others that is similar to a mother's for her child. Like the mother, we have a deep desire for others to have the very best. Of course, we are concerned that they have food, shelter, comfort, and their other basic needs, but we want much more for them than that. Many people have all their basic needs met, many have even fulfilled a lot of their desires, but how many people are truly content? How many feel they have everything they could ever want and at the same time aren't anxious about losing what they have? How many are completely free from painful emotions, such as aggression and attachment? How many have gone beyond all hopes and fears, including the fear of death? How many have achieved a supreme level of happiness that can't be diminished by any circumstances? If a mother knew that her child could have this kind of happiness, wouldn't that be her greatest wish for her child? What reason could she have to aim for anything less?

Every sentient being has the potential to achieve a state of complete, unwavering happiness without the slightest taint of suffering. This state, which is everyone's true nature and birthright, is what we mean when we use the word *enlightenment*. The universal potential to attain enlightenment isn't common knowledge. When we examine our own mind and see how much conflict and confusion there is, it may hardly seem possible that we could ever dwell in a state of unchanging peace and bliss. And when we look at some other people— or animals—it may seem even more far-fetched that they could have such potential.

On the other hand, the behavior of sentient beings proves that, deep down, we all sense this potential within ourselves. One of the Tibetan words for sentient beings is *drowa*, which literally means "moving." We are constantly moving toward what we feel will bring us happiness and away from what we feel will bring us suffering. Why are we all so heroically persistent, in spite of our long, tragic record of failure? It is because our intuition tells us that somehow we can still succeed. Intuitively we understand that the causes of our confusion and suffering can be removed. They are not intrinsic to our being. Intuitively, all sentient beings sense their own enlightened nature and know that there is a way to merge with and awaken to that nature.

This deep intelligence, thickly obscured as it is, drives us every moment of our lives. It is why sentient beings never stop moving. It is why we never give up. In this sense, we can say that all of us are striving for enlightenment. Right now, some may be traveling on a direct and efficient path, while others may be wandering blindly and pathetically, but we all long to reach the same destination.

If you understand that the deepest desire of all beings is to awaken to their true nature, then what is the vastest and noblest aspiration you can make for yourself? It is to become a perfect guide who can help all these beings—every last one of them—attain enlightenment. And how can you become a perfect guide? The only way is to attain enlightenment yourself.

When you awaken to your true nature, you will realize the same level of tsewa as the Buddha, who cares for all sentient beings like a mother for her only child. Along with seeing your tsewa fully blossom, you will also realize the complete blossoming of your knowledge and your power to benefit others. With these qualities, you will be a perfect guide.

The wish to attain enlightenment in order to guide all other beings to enlightenment is called *bodhichitta*, a Sanskrit word meaning "mind-set of awakening." Those who live by bodhichitta, who devote their time, energy, and passion to this altruistic quest, are known as bodhisattvas. As soon as we orient our own hearts in this way, we too start to become bodhisattvas. Even with all our present neuroses and confusion, we are eligible to walk on the bodhisattva path. The only qualification is having the seed of tsewa.

Finally, when this path brings us to complete maturity, when we realize our full potential, we are enlightened. We are *buddha*, which means "awakened one." The historical Buddha lived in India twenty-five hundred years ago, where he demonstrated the path to enlightenment and the qualities one obtains as a result. When you and I become buddhas, our mind and heart will be no different from this sublime being's.

When you are a buddha and you look back on your evolution, you will see where it all came from—the seed of tsewa, the very same tender heart that you already know. Chandrakirti spells it out: "Buddhas come from bodhisattvas, bodhisattvas come from bodhichitta, and bodhichitta comes from tsewa." This is why the great philosopher honors tsewa with his highest homage.

3

THE TENDER HEART IS WATER

Although all sentient beings are endowed with the tender heart of tsewa, very few are fortunate enough to realize how significant that is. How common is it for people to recognize their own tender heart as a seed that can grow into the tree of enlightenment? How common is it even for people to tap into their warm heart and realize how much better they feel when it is open than when it is closed? Even this simple observation is rare. Most of the time, the seed remains a seed.

We are in a different position, however. This is not because we are intrinsically superior to others, so we have no reason to be arrogant. But we do have the rare good fortune to have encountered a wisdom tradition that understands what tsewa is and how to make the most of it.

In ancient times, people would risk their lives to go on long ocean voyages in search of a magical jewel that was said to fulfill all wishes. Little did they know that the wish-fulfilling jewel was already in their own heart. Thanks to our fortunate connection to the enlightened beings in this world, we have some knowledge of the wish-fulfilling jewel in our heart. We know how to identify it. We know how to discern when it is actively bringing about its magical benefit and when it is lying dormant.

An acorn can't germinate on its own. It depends on other factors. If you put it in the glove compartment of your car, nothing will happen, even if you wait a thousand years. But if you plant it and attend to it, that tiny acorn can turn into a magnificent oak tree. If you had such a promising acorn and the perfect field in which to plant it, wouldn't it be a waste just to leave it in your glove compartment?

As much as it would be a shame to waste the potential of an acorn, how much more of a shame would it be to waste the potential of your tender heart? Since this seed, if properly cared for, is destined to grow into buddhahood, it is our duty to cultivate it. If we, who have knowledge of tsewa, don't do this, who else will? Therefore, it is our responsibility to make the most of our good fortune and become perfect guides to lead others to enlightenment. Otherwise we will be letting down humanity. We will be letting down all sentient beings, because all of them need a perfect guide to help them realize their own enlightened nature.

So how do we cultivate our seed of tsewa? Or, to continue with Chandrakirti's metaphors, what is the water that helps tsewa grow? That water is also tsewa. Now some may take this as an instruction to be passive. If we have a seed that waters itself, what is there for us to do? But it's clear that doing nothing won't get us anywhere. Though everyone has the tender heart, most of us are wandering in confusion, experiencing wave after wave of suffering in different forms. Most of us are like flies trapped indoors, longing to get out into the open air but crashing, over and over again, into the window.

For our water of tsewa to nurture our seed of tsewa, our own intention has to be involved. Intention is the most powerful ability that human beings have. But for this intention to lead to positive results, it has to be imbued with wisdom. How do we acquire this wisdom? It is by actively applying our innate critical intelligence to discern the truth. In this case, the truth is the unsurpassable value of tsewa. This is not a religious or dogmatic "truth"; it is something we can come to through our experience and our reasoning.

In this process, we will have a lot of help. We haven't yet discerned this truth fully, but the enlightened beings of the past and present have. They have made things easy for us with their thorough examination of the wonders of the warm, tender heart. They have tested their findings over and over again to arrive at a state of unshakable confidence.

But although much of the work has already been done for us, we still have to use our own experience to arrive at our own unshakable confidence. We have to observe our heart, over and over again, both when it's open and when it's closed. We have to contrast the experience of tsewa with the experience of being absorbed in our small self. We have to attend to and contemplate our tender heart until we value it as the enlightened ones do—until we value tsewa above all other things.

As we learn to value tsewa more and more, it becomes easier and easier for us to set a clear intention to cultivate it. And once we have set a clear, stable intention—a vision that stays with us continually, playing a role in everything we do—then much of our work has already been done. What is the most difficult part of the path to enlightenment? It is nothing more than our ongoing confusion about how to direct our intentions. So we can do ourselves a big favor by clarifying our intentions as soon as possible.

This will be easier for some than for others. Some people quickly grasp the significance of keeping the heart open and allowing tsewa to flow naturally and blissfully. They instinctively trust their tsewa to be the most reliable means of bringing happiness to themselves and others. And it makes intuitive sense to them that their fortunate situation gives them the responsibility to attain enlightenment for the benefit of all beings.

Other people have to do more investigating to convince themselves. They may have to spend a lot of time comparing the different states of their heart—open versus closed—until they have connected the dots and arrived at a place of certainty. They may have to learn the hard way, by proving to themselves repeatedly that looking for some kind of happiness outside of the warm heart is doomed to failure. It may take a lot of effort to reach the simple conclusion that having tsewa alone is enough to make their deepest wishes come true. And they may have a hard time envisioning their own tender heart bringing such vast and profound benefit to others.

The first type is not necessarily better than the second. The one who has to struggle more at first may end up with a more stable conviction because it is grounded in a more thorough process of reasoning. But whichever category you're in, I urge you to work toward setting a clear intention to bring tsewa into focus as the top priority of your life. Please direct the potential of your tender heart into bodhichitta, the wish to attain enlightenment in order to guide others there. If you can set that intention today, wonderful. If you need more time to examine these teachings and your experience, please take the time you need. The point is to arrive at this clear intention—this vision—which will make the rest of the path so much more straightforward.

This compassionate vision, which springs from the tender heart, is the water that enables the seed to sprout and grow. And just as an acorn needs water continually as it grows up from a sprout to a giant oak tree, we must continually maintain our noble intention. All the buddhas and bodhisattvas were at one time ordinary sentient beings just like ourselves. It was the compassionate vision of bodhichitta that inspired them to pursue the activities of the bodhisattva in training: to be giving, to abide in ethical discipline, to be tolerant, to concentrate on what is most important, and to explore the deepest wisdom concerning the ultimate truth—all with the great diligence that comes naturally from tsewa. Their warm heart, with its naturally flowing affection for others, was what kept them moving forward through all the stages and challenges of the path over the course of many lifetimes. It prevented them from becoming discouraged, from losing their zeal. Mothers, by their very nature, never give up on the well-being of their children. Similarly, if we clearly establish bodhichitta in our hearts, we will never give up on benefiting sentient beings, until every single one has realized their true nature, their own enlightened mind.

4

REMOVING IMPEDIMENTS TO TSEWA: THE MIND IN CRISIS

The practices taught by the Buddha don't create qualities in our minds that were not already present. If we didn't innately possess wisdom and the tender heart, there would be no way for us develop them. Wisdom and tsewa are not like goods we can import. The Dharma is not an import system; rather, it works by clearing away all that obscures our enlightened mind and its potential. Therefore, the principal method of the Dharma is to remove impediments.

There is a simple way to tap into the experience of tender heart and see how tsewa already dwells within you. Take a few quiet moments and recall five times in your life when you felt touched by someone's love and warmth toward you. Then remember five times when you expressed this kind of tenderness to someone else. This exercise will bring back some feeling of that open heart. Even though you are thinking about the past, you are experiencing tsewa in the present. The flow of tsewa is happening right now.

Tapping in to our tender heart is a wonderful practice that can help us develop trust in tsewa as the source of our deepest well-being. But merely tapping in from time to time will not lead us to experiencing the full potential of tsewa. Ultimately, we aspire to have a stable experience of tsewa, not a constant fluctuation between open and closed heart. But if it is so much more enjoyable for our heart to be open, why does it close in the first place? Why would we deprive ourselves of oxygen, not just once in a while, but regularly? The reason is that we have unhealthy mental habits, many of which are unconscious.

One of the most basic unhealthy habits is that we easily let our mind get disturbed. Since a disturbed mind is a poor atmosphere for tsewa, we need to create favorable conditions intentionally for our mind to be more clear and calm. It's amazing to see how different our mind can seem when it's relatively still. Getting to this state may involve sitting on a meditation cushion, or going to a park bench during our lunch break. An effective method is to sit still, count twenty-one breaths, and then look into our heart. This will create a good atmosphere in our mind. If we do this regularly, we will become better at noticing when our mind is becoming disturbed and our heart is starting to shut down. Gradually, this will help change our habitual pattern of getting thrown off so easily. Then our self-imposed suffering of oxygen deprivation will become less inevitable. But this all has to begin with a clear intention to create a favorable state of mind. If we simply leave it to chance, the tendency to get disturbed again and again will win out.

Of course, even if we diligently make the time to cultivate a clear mind, our time on the cushion or park bench will have to come to an end. We will have no choice but to face situations where our mind is likely to become disturbed. It will be harder to keep our heart open, with tsewa flowing abundantly. But we're not helpless; there are ways to limit how disturbed we get. Just because we live in a complicated world doesn't mean we have to throw in the towel and forget about tsewa altogether.

The human mind is endowed with two mechanisms that are its greatest protectors: mindfulness and vigilant introspection. *Mindfulness* means being aware of what's going on in your mind and heart. In this context, it refers to keeping a close watch on whether your heart is open or closed. *Vigilant introspection* means knowing how much is at stake. By learning to connect the dots of cause and effect, you start to appreciate how much difference tsewa makes to your well-being. You understand how important it is to pay attention to your heart at all times and to take appropriate measures when you notice it shutting down.

Mindfulness and vigilant introspection enable us to keep to our intentions and accomplish what we set out to do. Without them, none of the buddhas ever would have attained enlightenment. Without them, we will not be able to avoid the many pitfalls of the modern world. We can develop these two faculties by continually self-reflecting and observing our heart honestly and objectively. When we fully appreciate tsewa and clearly see how our happiness depends on it, then we will naturally be motivated to be vigilant about potential impediments to tsewa.

For example, when we're actively engaged in the world, one of the most common impediments is the habit of feeling like we're in a crisis. This problem is prevalent in modern life; there always seems to be some kind of major or minor crisis going on, at least in our thoughts and emotions. Sometimes there is an actual external crisis coming from outside ourselves. We are not denying that. But in other cases, we should honestly ask ourselves how much of the current crisis is our own creation.

We often generate a crisis to keep our minds occupied. Why would we do this to ourselves, when it is so unpleasant and also blocks the flow of warmth from our heart? My feeling is that we create many of these crises because we're unable to relax. We can't relax because we don't trust our good fortune. Something always seems wrong, so we have to keep stirring things up. Trusting our good fortune is easier said than done. It requires effort. But if we take time to contemplate the lives that most people and animals on this planet have to endure, we will see how our own lives are nearly perfect in comparison. Of course, we all suffer misfortunes and tragedies. At the very least, we don't get many things we want, and we do get many things we don't want. But when we objectively compare our lives to those of the vast majority, it will become obvious how fortunate we are.

If we make a concerted effort to think about and appreciate each blessing we have, rather than go the more common route of tallying our misfortunes, we will feel enriched and more at ease. We will have less desire to get busy and solve self-created problems or to elevate something small into something that feels like a matter of life and death. Instead, we will learn to depend on tsewa as our most reliable source of happiness. We will even come to see our "misfortunes" as helpful. For if we got everything we wanted in life, we would find ourselves trapped in a bubble of self-absorption. We would be cut off from others and disconnected from reality. We would have no noble, altruistic purpose in life—no motivation to pursue the path of enlightenment for the benefit of all sentient beings.

But even if we do learn to see how our lives are nearly perfect in the present, we still have to overcome another source of tremendous anxiety—the future. How do we know our good fortune will last? Didn't the Buddha say that everything is impermanent? Couldn't there be some disaster lurking around the corner?

It's true that you have no idea what's around the corner. You don't have control over all the events that could take place in your life. But you do have control of the general trajectory. If you make the tender heart your highest priority, your mind will feel more and more at ease, more and more in harmony with the world. You will find that as you express more warmth toward others, they will express more warmth toward you. Your world will become an increasingly friendly place. As this happens, your trust that tsewa is indeed a wish-fulfilling jewel will grow. Then you will find less reason to struggle and less reason to be anxious.

It is said that there are four ways we can travel into the future: from light to light, from light to darkness, from darkness to light, and from darkness to darkness. We have the option to be in the first category. We are already in a state of light because we have an innately tender heart and the knowledge and means to continue developing our tsewa. Then, as we go into the future motivated by bodhichitta, the wish to attain enlightenment for the benefit of all beings, we can be sure that this light will only increase. And even when we do encounter hardships and misfortunes—such as the inevitable phases of old age, sickness, and death—our tsewa will give us the resilience to make the best of our suffering and use it to open our heart even further.

If we contemplate our present and future in these ways, we can remain cheerful even in the face of temporary difficulties. But if we lose our perspective and go along with our habitual momentum, we are likely to create a continual sequence of crises as we go through life. Reacting to our constantly nagging anxiety, we will keep ourselves in a turbulent state of mind. This can be a form of addiction. The "benefit" of this unconscious strategy is that when our mind is already turbulent, we feel less concerned about any further turbulence that could occur. Keeping our mind stirred up helps us avoid dealing directly with our fears and anxieties. By amplifying our current problems, we temporarily forget about the bigger issues down the road, such as major losses and death.

This whole approach ends up backfiring because a mind in constant crisis is not a hospitable environment for tsewa. We may be distracting ourselves from our greater fears, but we are also distracting ourselves from our only reliable source of happiness. The remedy for this habit is to keep close watch on our mind and, if we see ourselves going toward the turbulence, to turn our attention in a more positive direction by cultivating trust in our good fortune. Doing so, we will have more opportunity to develop our tender heart, and we will be able to progress quickly.

5

OPENING THE INJURED HEART

Another of the most common impediments to tsewa is holding a grudge. If someone has caused you pain, it's challenging
to keep your heart open to that person. Even worse, a grudge
against one person or a few people can turn into a much bigger form of resentment, such as prejudice toward an entire
group of people or animosity toward the entire human race.
It's not uncommon for a few experiences of being hurt to
block all flow of tenderness from a person's inherently warm
heart.

If you shut down your heart because of past injuries, life
becomes a painful ordeal. Even if you hold a grudge against
just one person, anytime you think of them, or recall the
time you were hurt, you will suffer. Since you have no control
over when these thoughts will arise in your mind, you will always be susceptible to sudden pain. And if you resent many

people, whole groups of people, or humanity at large, you will be that much more susceptible. It will be like walking around a crowded train station in India with an open wound. There is no peace in such an existence, no matter how good your life may look from the outside.

To let go of our grudges, we must understand that we are not stuck with them. We have two choices. The habitual option is to keep holding on—to keep depriving ourselves of the oxygen of tsewa. The other way is to make whatever effort it takes to let go and thereby restore the naturally exuberant flow of love to our heart. We may believe we're protecting our heart by shutting it down, but that is a confused way of thinking. Trying to protect ourselves in this way ends up being what harms us the most. There is a classic analogy: If an arrow wounds you, you can blame the one who shot the arrow for your injury. But if you then take that arrow and grind it deeper and deeper into your wound, that is your own doing.

The past is important, but not as important as the present and the future. The past has already been lived. It doesn't have to be relived. To sacrifice the present and the future by reliving past injuries is not the way of the sages. When we find ourselves caught in a grudge, we should notice how we are perpetuating the past. Something has happened, and we have put together a whole story around it that we repeat to ourselves over and over like a broken record. And we tend to be so stubborn about these stories: "This is what happened, and there's no other way of looking at it." In this way, we continue to grind the arrow into the wound. Our mind and heart are frozen around this issue. How can we breathe our oxygen of tsewa in such a state?

Closing our heart because of a grudge doesn't harm only ourselves. Our negativity affects the people around us, such as our family and friends and those who depend on us. It makes it harder for them to be close to us, to feel relaxed in our presence. Though we may not act out with physical and mental abuse, our internal unhappy state distresses others, especially our children, who can perceive us in a less conceptual, more energetic way. On the other hand, overcoming our resentments and fully reclaiming our innate tsewa—our birthright to feel love and tenderness toward all—brings tremendous benefit to others. In the present, those around us feel our warmth, which in turn induces their own tsewa to flow. And in the long term, our tender heart is the seed of realizing our full potential to benefit others by attaining enlightenment.

Some grudges are easy to overcome, but with others, it may seem almost impossible to let go. Perhaps someone has let us down again and again. Perhaps someone we were kind to has hurt us badly. Perhaps someone has been cruel to us and shown no remorse. But whoever these individuals are and whatever they did, we have to keep in mind the bigger picture of what's at stake: our wish-fulfilling jewel of tsewa. Sometimes it takes a lot of work to overcome resentment, but we are capable of doing that work as long as we are motivated. And we will be motivated as long as we understand there's no good alternative.

For encouragement, we can look at examples such as Mahatma Gandhi, Martin Luther King Jr., Nelson Mandela, and His Holiness the Dalai Lama. These people, and countless men and women who are not well known, prove that we can keep our hearts open toward all sentient beings without exception, even those who have hurt us or are committed to being against us. They have shown us that it's possible to remain cheerful and strong in the most difficult conditions.

We may believe that these heroic people are inherently different from us. Unlike us, we may think, they have divine strength or some magical ingredient in their minds that makes it possible to forgive. But that ingredient is nothing other than innate, universal tsewa. We have that same source of strength and forgiveness in our own tender heart. It's true that these great people have been able to put their tsewa to greater use than we have, but in our potential, we are no different.

We might think that such strength in maintaining the flow of tsewa is not "normal" for human beings. It is normal to have aversion, at the very least, toward those who threaten or harm us. The fact that the Dalai Lama is not bitter or mean-spirited toward those who have harmed him and his people, but instead feels warmly toward them, strikes us as somehow beyond the normal—and it is. Most people would be damaged in some way by such suffering, but for His Holiness, painful experiences have only brought him more in touch with his most reliable source of happiness. The Dharma teaches us that we all have the potential to keep our hearts continually warm with a love that is more than normal, that goes beyond how people view us or treat us. Instead of being tied up with our attachments, as is the case with "normal" love, tsewa is based on the free and natural expression of an unimpeded heart. Therefore, when we fully harness the power of tsewa, there is no misfortune or aversion that can block its warmth from flowing.

When it comes to forgiveness, how you identify yourself is crucial. If you identify yourself as an injured person bound to your grudge, you will be stuck in that self-created prison. But that poor victim is not who you truly are. When your confusion is stripped away and your tsewa is allowed to flow freely and exuberantly, you will find in yourself the same courage and equanimity as the Dalai Lama or Dr. King. This is true for all of us without exception, for the ability to forgive and move on is one of the many gifts of tsewa.

Keeping your heart closed toward others who have hurt you is the natural result of perpetuating your negative story lines. It can seem like a satisfying way of repaying the injury. Perhaps unconsciously, you are thinking, "This person did this to me, so I'm going to get him back by maintaining a cold grudge in my heart." Maybe your negative thoughts will make your enemy suffer. Maybe he will even come to you and beg for forgiveness on his knees! But even if your "best-case scenario" miraculously occurs, will it restore the mental and emotional balance you've lost while depriving yourself of tsewa? Will it bring you the peace and joy you long for every moment of your existence? Or will you have just caused yourself a lot of extra suffering that continues to disturb you like a hangover? And if the improbable desired outcome of your story never happens, how long are you willing to keep grinding the arrow into your wound?

These are questions you must ask yourself in your darkest hour, sincerely and objectively. Being objective will require you to step aside from your emotions and prejudices and look at the bigger picture. If you have observed the glories of the tender heart in your own experience, how does the possibility of fulfilling your story line compare? How does it compare to watering the seed of tsewa and watching it grow and grow until you realize your potential to become a buddha? Would you really prefer to collapse into your small, contracted self and its relatively minor concerns? Would you like that to be the dominant habit of your mind and heart?

If we ask ourselves these questions, we will inevitably conclude that keeping our heart closed is an unproductive way of working with our stories. A more intelligent way is to put the story in a bigger context. What is the one fact about every sentient being that never changes? It is our constant wish to be happy and free from suffering. The infinite differences in how we appear and how we behave are all temporary because they come from temporary conditions. Almost all of these conditions are beyond our control. They are based on other temporary conditions, which are based on more conditions, and so on. But underneath this limitless display of interdependence, we are all the same. No one is permanently one way or another—good or bad, right or wrong, for us or against us.

When we hold a grudge, however, we see everything through the lens of that resentment. We see other beings, who are equal to us at the core, as intrinsically selfish, inconsiderate, or just plain bad. They can even appear to us as permanent enemies.

Right now we may be having a lot of turmoil around one particular person. If so, we should ask ourselves, "Has it always been this way with them? If not, then what has changed? Have they really changed at the core? Or is it that temporary conditions have changed? Will it always be this way in the future, or does that also depend on temporary conditions?"

We will quickly realize that people and our relationships with them are always changing. There is no malevolent, unchanging person who has always been and will always be against us. So if the conditions are responsible for what has gone wrong, does it make sense to hold on to blame? The object of our grudge is, in fact, quite innocent, like a child. He or she only wants to be happy and free from suffering but unfortunately sabotages these desires out of ignorance. If we were under the same conditions, we would be acting in the same confused way. In fact, we ourselves, though we may be well educated in the Dharma, also can't help harming others from time to time because of our own conditions. No sentient being is exempt from wrongdoing. But no one is intrinsically bad either. This is how we can understand things when we're not blinded by our resentment.

From the Buddhist teachings' point of view, nothing happens by chance. Every effect has its causes. This is the law of karma. Sometimes the relationship between cause and effect is immediate and obvious. You drop a glass and it breaks. You don't sleep enough and you feel lousy. Sometimes karma is a little more subtle but still observable. We may need someone to point out the cause and effect so we can study it in our own experience until we are convinced. A good example here is tsewa. When our heart is open, we feel joy. When it's closed, we feel pain. This is how karma works.

In the majority of cases, however, karma is too intricate and far-reaching for ordinary beings like ourselves to be able to comprehend it fully. To use some classic Buddhist examples, we don't know why peas are round or why peacocks' tails have iridescent eyes. But just because our vision is too limited to trace back a vast array of causes doesn't mean things happen at random. If they did, then why would farmers plant seeds and expect crops to grow? Why would we do anything and expect a result? A mixture of karma and randomness is also illogical. For how would it make sense for some things to happen due to cause and effect and other things to happen by pure chance? Chance is just an illusion. We say that a roll of the dice is "random" because there is no way for anyone to predict the outcome. But is it truly random? No, there are clearly causes leading to a result. There is no such thing in this universe as genuine randomness.

If you hurt someone, it's natural for them to want to repay the injury. So if they hurt you back, at some point you will probably understand where they're coming from—unless you remain caught up in strong emotions or keep justifying your previous action. When you wise up to the mutually destructive pattern and its potential to go on and on, you will be in a good position to realize the best course of action: to open your heart and put an end to the cycle by forgiving.

Here is one powerful technique for opening your heart toward someone against whom you hold a grudge. This works by tapping into the kindness and joy that already arise in the course of your life. When you notice yourself feeling tenderness toward another being—your parent, your child, a friend, a pet—bring to mind the person you resent. Then, with one sudden movement of your mind, see if you can transfer your warm feeling to that person. This abrupt shift can short-circuit your story line and establish conditions in your mind to feel more open toward the object of your bitterness. Of course, this technique and any other will only work for those who really want to get over their grudges.

In some cases, you may feel more justified in holding on to your resentment. For example, what about when someone causes you pain and you feel like you've done nothing to deserve it? This is a good time to think about the vastness of karma. Who you are and what you experience in this life is infinitely varied and complex. The story of your life includes your physical and mental attributes, your habits and preferences, the people around you, the places you inhabit and visit, countless events, good and bad fortune, and so much more. Could all the causes of this intricate web of detail be located within the few decades since your birth? And what about the causes of those causes, and so on? Wouldn't this be a severely limited way of looking at things?

For this and many other reasons, it makes sense to expand our story to include past and future lives. When we do so, we find much more room in our heart for forgiveness. Looking at just this one life, it appears that the reason someone hurt us has nothing to do with our own past actions. We are the victim, the other person is the culprit. That's the whole story—and that's where we're stuck. But when we have confidence that nothing happens at random, we can be sure that at some point in the past the roles were reversed: we were the culprit, and the other person was the victim. Otherwise, why would this particular person out of so many have come to have this relationship with us? For anything that happens to us, we must have been involved in the past, whether we can trace it back or not.

The point of reflecting on karma in this way is not to make ourselves feel guilty. Karma is not some form of divine punishment for our sins. There's no one in charge of this process: it's just how things naturally work. No one "deserves" pain and suffering. But at the same time, our relationships don't just pop up out of a void. If we don't understand or acknowledge how things actually function, our view of the world will be distorted. Every victim in this world has been a culprit, and every culprit a victim. Every prey has been a predator, and every predator prey. This cyclic pattern in which we all cause and experience pain is known as *samsara*. The cause of samsara itself is ignorance of our true nature, which includes the true nature of our heart—tsewa. From this point of view, the entire point of the path to enlightenment is to gain the wisdom that will help ourselves and others go beyond this cycle.

If our aim is enlightenment—or at least some form of spiritual growth—then any time we are hurt, we can view it as an opportunity. Now we have a chance to look at things in a different way, which is based on wisdom. We can choose not to see the story with ourselves in the role of intrinsic victim and the other person in the role of intrinsic culprit. Both of us have the wish-fulfilling jewel of the tender heart, which gives us the potential to attain the ultimate state of happiness. But both of us, perhaps to different degrees, have let our jewel go to waste because of our ignorance. Either we haven't recognized our tsewa, we haven't appreciated it, or we've failed to take advantage of it because we continually get swept away by our habits. So far, our impediments have gotten the best of us. That is why we keep hurting one another. But now that we've encountered the Buddha's wisdom and skillful means, we can finally learn to open our heart to all, including those who have hurt us in this life. As we gain confidence in the power of our tsewa, we can even hold a special place in our heart for the former objects of our grudges. We can be grateful that they have helped to open our eyes to the cyclic nature of suffering and motivated us to expand our mind and try a different approach. And if they are continuing to hurt others out of the suffering of a closed heart, we can feel compassion for them. In this way, the pain we have gone through can be transformed from an impediment into a warm rain that nourishes our precious seed of tsewa.

Another self-destructive story we may tell ourselves when we've been hurt is that our open heart itself was the cause of our suffering. This is a common scenario in romantic love, for example. In the beginning, our love is so innocent and trusting, but when things don't work out the way we had hoped, we can become bitter and jaded about love itself. We can blame love for our hurt and then have a hard time opening our heart toward others. But love is never the culprit. An open heart only provides joy, never suffering. If a few experiences of being disappointed make us give up on love altogether, our world will become dark and gloomy, even if everything else in our life works out the way we want. Therefore, to avoid this outcome, we have to investigate what has really happened, setting our story lines aside as much as possible. We need to look at cause and effect objectively, until we are able to blame whatever deserves blame—whether it's our unreasonable attachments, our expectations, or our lack of wisdom and skillful means. When we use our mind to prove love not guilty in this way, then our heart will once again be free to love—from one person, to many people, and eventually to all sentient beings.

A similar descent into jadedness can happen with children as they grow up. Young children who are brought up in good circumstances feel a lot of love for their parents, for the world, for their games and activities, and so on. They maintain this innocent openness until they get older and meet the complex reality of the world. Then the innocent phase comes to an end, and they are faced with a challenge. At this point, they need to develop wisdom to keep that warm feeling flowing in the heart. Otherwise, they may interpret their loss of innocence as evidence that they have awakened from some kind of self-delusion: "Now it is time to wake up and accept the grim facts of life, the harsh reality of the world," they may think. With such thoughts, it is natural for them to feel foolish about their naïveté and gullibility, and they may blame their disappointment on their openness of heart. The world is indeed full of harsh realities, but that is no justification for shutting down into our small, bitter self. On the contrary, the painful nature of samsara is the most important reason for us to find ways to keep our hearts continually warm with tsewa.

To reopen our heart after a deep hurt or a painful disillusionment can take a long time, even if we understand how necessary it is to do so. Even when we apply the effective methods of the Dharma, such as those mentioned earlier, we may find that our thoughts still return to whatever self-destructive story we were telling ourselves. Because we have given a lot of energy to perpetuating these stories, there will still be momentum for them to keep resurfacing and occasionally carry us away. We have to be patient with this process. In our mind, thoughts are continually arising and dissolving, arising and dissolving. The thoughts that make up the story behind our injured heart are no different. But if we just give these thoughts space to arise and dissolve, they will eventually wear themselves out. The story will lose its feeling of reality and it will no longer be able to convince us. The key here is to focus on our tender heart and not pay so much attention to the story. If we do so, our tsewa eventually will overcome our confused and limited way of looking at things. We will have more confidence in tsewa and thus more confidence in ourselves. This confidence will be invaluable in carrying us forward along our spiritual journey.

Although they may take a long time to let go of completely, the most painful forms of grudge or disappointment can be the easiest for us to make progress with. The acute pain they cause gives us a lot of incentive to work with them. But in addition to these more blatant hurts, we can hold on to other forms of resentment that also block the flow of tsewa from our heart.

One of the most common causes of resentment is when we feel our love and tenderness are not reciprocated. It's as if our tsewa comes with an implied condition—we can continue to keep our heart open only if the other party meets this expectation. This is not to say that reciprocation isn't important. Gratitude, appreciation, and the willingness to reciprocate are signs of good character. Those who are strong in these qualities are well respected, and deservedly so. Also, mutual reciprocation gives people a greater sense of solidarity with each other.

But none of this should make reciprocation a condition for our expressing tsewa. Parents are able to love their young children, even before good character has formed. If parents always needed reciprocation, they couldn't even begin parenthood. After all, babies do not reciprocate. We hope that our children will eventually become mature enough to know the value of gratitude and become worthy of our respect in this way. But until then, we never even think of making reciprocation a requirement.

When it comes to expressing our tender heart, we should try to have the same openness and tolerance that parents have with small children. This openness is based on appreciating tsewa as the source of all happiness, including our own. As the great sage Shantideva said, "If you make yourself a delicious meal, will you expect gratitude from yourself?" If you apply your power of discernment to your experience, you will see how tsewa is its own reward and how keeping your heart filled with tenderness is itself the greatest joy. If others respond well to your warmth, that is a bonus, but the continued flow of your tsewa shouldn't be based on the response.

If we can't recognize the joy in tsewa, it's easy for us to get confused about why we are keeping our heart open. Are we doing it because we want to be good, because we're "supposed to be" loving and compassionate? Are we doing it because of our ideas about karma, or because we've made some kind of commitment or vow? Are we doing it in response to some kind of pressure? If any of these become our primary motivation for expressing tsewa, then we may well overlook how joyful it is to have a tender heart. Our love will be based on concepts, not on our deep, heartfelt connection to the source of everything positive in the world.

Sometimes we don't open our heart to others because we feel they are unworthy of our tender feelings. We are full of love and warmth, we think, but not everyone deserves our tsewa. Some people aren't pure enough vessels to merit our outpouring of love and affection. They lack this or that qualification. If we are not careful, our critical mind will come up with a long list of requirements. Then our tsewa, which has the potential to flow limitlessly, will be walled in by our biases. That is not intelligence; it is ignorance. When we let the natural expression of our tender heart be handcuffed to a set of qualifications, we are putting our small, confused self in charge. We are forgetting that all beings are equally in need of tsewa because all beings—ourselves included—are constantly longing to be happy and free from suffering.

We are also forgetting the equality of all beings when we allow prejudices to tighten our heart. We may block our tsewa because of religion, gender, nationality, cultural differences, political differences, race, species, and so on. These prejudices can be very subtle, manifesting as a slight contraction or a feeling of indifference. They may not stand out as anything worth noticing, much less remedying. But these subtle blockages hinder our tsewa, and thus hinder our own happiness and our path to enlightenment. Therefore, we need to apply continual mindfulness and vigilant introspection to make sure we don't come under the sway of any form of prejudice.

We need to be wary of closing our heart not only with people we know or encounter, but even with those we have never met or seen in person. It seems natural to withhold tsewa from a corrupt politician or ruthless war criminal that we read about in the news. But by doing so, we reverse our progress toward realizing the full capacity of our tender heart. Even if all our friends, or all of society, supports our closing down toward certain "evil" people, we have to put things in proper perspective, remembering the law of karma and choosing to have a bigger view of things. Otherwise, we won't be able to arouse genuine bodhichitta, the aspiration to attain enlightenment for the benefit of all beings without exception.

The great Tibetan teacher Dromtönpa was once circumambulating a temple with a few of his disciples. Circumambulation is a traditional practice of showing respect to an object of veneration. At the outer edge of the circumambulation path, a stray dog was lying on the ground. Instead of walking down the middle of the path, Dromtönpa purposely went around the dog so as to include it in the circle of veneration. When one of his disciples asked him why he was paying such respect to a stray dog, Dromtönpa said, "I'm not paying respect to a dog. I'm paying respect to a being whose nature is enlightened." This is how a sage sees other beings. However they may temporarily appear or behave, all sentient beings have the seed of enlightenment in their tender heart. Their innate tsewa may be thickly obscured, but it is still there. If we look at things from a wider perspective, we will know that there is something to venerate in everyone.

Our biases can come up not only in giving tsewa, but in receiving it as well. Sometimes we only want to receive tenderness and support from special people, an exclusive group that is worthy of giving that to us. But we are not like flowers that can only blossom if they receive rays of light from the sun.

That is too limited a view. We can blossom by receiving tsewa from anyone, from the highest to the lowest. If we are too picky about whom we receive warmth from, then we may even lose the affection of those we do admit to our heart. For it will become harder and harder for the latter to meet our standards and expectations.

Sometimes we turn away from others' tsewa because we are suspicious. Why is this person being so nice to me? What's behind his friendly expressions? This person doesn't even know me. What could he want? Is he planning to take advantage of me? So much paranoia can manifest when someone spontaneously and genuinely tries to be friendly with us. Of course, people can have ulterior motives, but 99 percent of the time, they are simply expressing the natural human desire to connect with one another. Why turn that into something else, something from which we need to protect ourselves?

If we let the 1 percent spoil the other 99 percent, we are letting our suspiciousness color all our relations. On one hand, we always long for love in our lives. We know we can't be happy if we isolate ourselves. But on the other hand, we feel that we're taking a big risk by opening up to receive tsewa. We have to recognize that this risk—which is usually tiny—is a risk well worth taking. What do we think we have to lose? Whatever it could be, that loss is nothing compared to the pain of keeping our heart closed in fear and paranoia.

At other times, we may feel that we just don't deserve love. Somehow we're fake, and when our true colors are exposed, we'll be rejected. Inside we may feel shaky and weak. In this state, it's very hard to open up to receiving warmth from any-body. This is when we have to remember that no one is un-deserving. We are no worse than the dog that Dromtönpa circumambulated. We are also no better—everyone has the same precious tsewa. There is nothing fake about what lies at the core of all our hearts. We may have a lot of negative habits and shameful thoughts, but they are not our true colors.

As you remove impediments to giving and receiving tsewa, your mind and your life will be transformed. As you let go of small-minded stories and biases, you will be more and more amazed at how much warmth there is in this world. You will find so many beings to whom you can reach out and so many who can touch you as well. Wherever you stay or go, you will be able to make a difference in many others' lives, and many others will be able to make a difference in your life. When you orient yourself to tsewa, what you can give and receive is boundless.

6

CLINGING TO THE SELF:
THE ROOT OF ALL IMPEDIMENTS

In the Dharma, we often speak about the "self" or "ego." Clinging to this self is said to be the source of all our suffering—and the source of samsara as a whole. When we cling to the self, we automatically feel the need to cherish and protect it. This inevitably leads to experiencing disturbing emotions, such as attachment, aggression, jealousy, arrogance, and stupidity. Driven by these emotions, we continually harm ourselves and others. This is the very formula for samsara. From this point of view, we can see how self-clinging is the opposite of the warm tenderness that naturally flows from an open heart. In fact, it is the root of all impediments to tsewa.

But before we make such claims, we should first look into what is meant by *self*. There are two main ways we can think about the self. First, we can say that the self is simply the one who experiences. Who is that? It can't be merely the body, because on its own, the body does not have any experience. At the moment of its conception, at the time the father's sperm fertilizes the mother's egg, the single-celled body is infused with consciousness. Without the addition of consciousness, even if the zygote divides successfully and somehow develops into a baby that can be born and grow to adulthood, there will be no one to experience life. It is our consciousness who experiences all the stages of this life and then continues to experience life after life. Our consciousness is the one who wanders in samsara and the one who finds liberation from samsara. As there is no denying this stream of experience, there is no denying a "self" who experiences. But this mere experiencer is not an impediment to tsewa or to anything else.

The self that causes all the problems is something much more than that which experiences. This self is an unconscious, habitual projection of the mind, without any reality. But even though it has no reality, we believe in it strongly, never questioning it. We identify with it and feel it is the most important thing in the universe. This intense, painful clinging to an illusion is the deeper reason we have so much trouble opening our tender heart. But by looking closely at how we project this illusory self, we can gradually free ourselves from our belief and attachment. Then there will be nothing to stop our innate tsewa from flowing exuberantly to all beings.

The illusory self with which we identify has three important characteristics. First of all, it is *singular*. For example, when you go to a train station, you buy one ticket. Even though you are made of many parts, you don't think of yourself as plural. When you refer to yourself, you refer to a single person: "me." Second, this illusory self is *unchanging*. Even though the body continually changes and the mindstream never remains the same for an instant, we have an unconscious belief in an underlying self that doesn't change. We think the "me" living now is essentially the same "me" who was born decades ago and that we will be the same "me" on our deathbed. Finally, we project a self that is *autonomous*. This means that it exists objectively on its own, independent of causes and conditions. We cling to a self that somehow exists separately from the rest of the world.

We can only be attached to a self if we project these three characteristics onto it. If we know the self isn't singular, unchanging, or autonomous, there is no way to identify with it. For example, if this self is composed of many parts, it makes no sense to be attached to it. We may think of this body as our self, but since the body is plural, which part or parts of it do we cling to? Or if we think of our mind as our self, which aspect of our mind? Our thoughts? Our feelings? Our perceptions? Which thoughts, feelings, or perceptions? The more we break things down and expose the true plural nature of this self, the more we realize that the whole process of clinging and identifying is a delusion.

Similarly, if we realize our continuously changing nature, we will also undermine our attachment to an illusory self. Why would we cling to something if we knew it never stayed the same? With which self would we identify—the self of today, or the self of tomorrow? The self of this morning, or the self of this afternoon? At a subtle level, the body changes every instant, and the mindstream never stops flowing. We can give a river a name such as "Ganges," but ultimately there is no one Ganges. It is an ever-transient display of phenomena, just like the body, the mind, and the "self."

Finally, it makes no sense to cling to something that doesn't exist autonomously. We project this self as an independent entity, but it only exists in relation to other things. The body depends on food, drink, warmth, and many other factors. Our thoughts, emotions, personality, and general sense of who we are depend on outer influences such as people and our environment. And everything we depend on depends, in turn, on countless other conditions, and so on. If we see that it's impossible to define a boundary between "self" and "other," how can we identify with a self? What would that self be?

On an intellectual level, it is easy to see that none of these three characteristics are absolutely true. It is obvious that there are many parts to a person. It is obvious that the body and mind are always changing. It is obvious that we are affected by the outer world. Yet emotionally we cling to a self in all three of these ways. Our unconscious emotional habits are much stronger than the concepts of our intellect. Even if we go through this analysis diligently, there is likely to be some lingering doubt. We can search high and low without finding anything singular, unchanging, and autonomous but still feel that there must be a self somewhere. So it is important to keep looking and to keep not finding until we are completely convinced.

Projecting a singular, unchanging, autonomous self is like being fooled by a scarecrow. If you drive by a cornfield at seventy miles per hour, you may think that what you're seeing is a man. Under those conditions, you are as ignorant as the average crow that gets scared away. But if you stop your car and get close enough to the scarecrow to see what it's really made of, your ignorance will evaporate.

Of course, realizing that a scarecrow is a scarecrow is much easier than fully realizing egolessness. Identifying with a multiple, changing, dependent collection of phenomena as a "self" is the most persistent misunderstanding we have. It has been with us not just for this lifetime, but for countless lives before this one. It is such a powerful delusion that we have never even had the curiosity to question it. So when we hear for the first time that this self doesn't exist, it can come as a shock. Even if we grasp the simple reasoning that shows how the self is like a scarecrow, it will take a while to fully assimilate the information. We will feel a lot of resistance to the idea: "Has all my attachment to myself been in vain? Has all my aggression to protect myself been in vain? Has all my jealousy and pride been in vain?"

But the news that the self is like a scarecrow is the best news we could possibly hear. When we recognize the self's illusory nature, we can stop paying so much attention to it. We can stop feeling so obliged to cherish and protect it. We can stop being so foolishly loyal to this all-consuming attachment. And we can stop undergoing the intense pain of all our self-centered emotions.

As the noble Atisha said, "The truly learned person is the one who knows that the self is a mental projection." Why is this the supreme knowledge? Because there is no worse tyranny than that of our self-centered emotions. Realizing self-lessness instantly frees us from this tyranny. Yes, when we look back, all of our attachment and aggression have indeed been in vain. Just like every other being in samsara, we have perpetually been barking up the wrong tree. But going forward, as we start to appreciate our egoless nature and cultivate the ability to let go of the illusory self, we will become more and more free from all of these vain emotions.

It is only possible to let go of the self when we realize there is no good reason to hold on. Identifying with a self is not necessary. It doesn't benefit us in any way. It's merely an ignorant habit. There is not even anything real to cling to. If there were a real self to cherish and protect, letting go of it would be like taking a baby away from its mother. But in this case, we are simply talking about letting go of a habitual misunderstanding. We have been under the power of this habit since before we can remember, and there is strong momentum for it to continue into the future. But that doesn't mean we can't overcome it. Because our own mind generated this habit, our own mind—now armed with the knowledge of the Dharma—can dismantle it as well. Any habit formed out of ignorance can be dismantled by wisdom.

If we take the time to look for this singular, unchanging, autonomous self that we empower to rule over our lives, we will gain clarity in the truth of egolessness, as well as confidence in our ability to overcome our deepest delusion. Looking for the self and not finding it is the gateway to liberation from suffering. We need to look and not find, not just once, but over and over again.

We need to do this examination not only in our quiet time of contemplation, but in our everyday life. For example, next time you are feeling a powerful emotion such as anger, pride, or insecurity, instead of simply struggling with the emotion, observe how that emotion is based on a strong sense of self. This sense of self is not something abstract. It is something you can feel. But then try to find that self. Really look for that self, in the ways I have described or in any other way you can think of. In the end, I predict you won't find a self that is singular, unchanging, and autonomous. You won't find a self worth clinging to. The Buddha couldn't find such a real self, so I don't think any of us will find one either.

When you can't find any self to hold on to, it becomes easy to let go. Even when strong emotions come up, you can let them be. You can let them arise and dissolve into space without reacting to them and reinforcing them. This is a more peaceful and effective process than suppressing the emotions or trying somehow to let go of them forcibly. Working with our emotions in such unnatural ways only solidifies our habit of cherishing and protecting the self. But when we work with the self directly—by looking and not finding—we wear away the ego-clinging habit of many lifetimes and at the same time gain freedom from all of that habit's side effects.

One of the most harmful side effects of identifying strongly with an illusory self is that it blocks the flow of our innate tsewa. But as we become more and more free from ignorance, we will find that our heart is filled more and more with warmth and love for others. When the primary impediment of self-clinging is removed, our heart will open naturally, on its own.

Now here, you may think, "If all beings have no self, who will be affected by the flow of tsewa from my heart? Who is longing for happiness and freedom from suffering? Who will benefit from my loving-kindness and compassion? Why is it meaningful to have tsewa?" From the ultimate point of view, it's true that there are no sentient beings to benefit. Nonetheless, projecting an illusory self and becoming attached to it produces an undeniable experience of suffering. When we start to come out of our deluded self-clinging and experience relief from our self-centered emotions, we feel even more empathy for all the beings who mistakenly identify with a scarecrow-like self. Ironically, the more we realize that all beings have no self, the more compassion we have for them.

A related question is how it is possible for us to benefit others when we are without a self. Chandrakirti answers this by referring to the example of the Buddha. No one has ever surpassed the Buddha in his realization of egolessness. But for the sake of communication, he said "I" and spoke of "my teachings." To relate to others, the Buddha adopted a functional self. For practical purposes, he designated the continuum of his body and mind as "I," while never *believing* in the reality of a singular, unchanging, autonomous self. Once the Buddha attained enlightenment, he was never again fooled by a mental projection, as all of us sentient beings are.

Enlightened beings such as the Buddha prove that we don't need to identify with a self to function beautifully and gloriously. All the ego does is get in the way. In the absence of delusion, there is still a mind, an experiencer. But this mind is our innate wisdom-mind, our enlightened nature, which is fully imbued with tsewa. When it is free from impediments, our wisdom-mind knows beyond a shadow of a doubt that tsewa is the true, unfailing cause of our own and others' well-being. When we overcome all traces of self-clinging, there is nothing to prevent our tsewa from spreading to all sentient beings unconditionally and impartially. There is nothing to prevent our tenderness from warming up the entire universe.

7

THE FRUIT OF TENDERNESS:
BENEFITING OTHERS

When we carefully and diligently water our seed of tsewa, applying all the wisdom and skillful means we can gather, that seed will eventually grow into a magnificent tree bearing abundant fruit. This is the third metaphor in Chandrakirti's homage to the tender heart. The fruit manifests as an ever-increasing desire and ability to benefit others.

We can benefit beings in many ways—physically, emotionally, mentally—and we should always take advantage of any opportunity we have to help others. But the greatest benefit of all, the one we should set our sights on, is to help others awaken completely to the inexhaustible tenderness of their own hearts. When we can help people achieve their full potential of tsewa—when their tsewa reaches the stage where it flows with the power and grace of Niagara Falls—we have benefited them in the profoundest way possible.

To achieve our full potential to benefit others in this way, we first have to do whatever it takes to open our own heart, further and further. As my mother used to say, "You have to make your heart so big you could hold a horse race inside of it." When your heart is as big as it could possibly be, big enough to hold deep love for every sentient being in the universe, then you have reached the full blossoming of your enlightened nature. Because you have shed every remnant of self-clinging, your mind is completely and forever free of delusion. There is nothing to obscure your understanding of how beings suffer and how their minds can be transformed. Like the Buddha, you have reached a state where you can be the perfect guide for others.

This doesn't mean that you will be able to bring others to enlightenment without their own effort being involved and regardless of all other conditions. As it is said, even the buddhas can't transport sentient beings to higher states of happiness as if tossing up a pebble. Everyone has their own impediments and their own karma. Even the most perfect guide can't intervene in someone else's karma and rearrange their life for them. If that were possible, it would already have happened for all of us, because the buddhas and bodhisattvas have no greater wish than to bring all beings to enlightenment.

Reflecting on this will give us a more realistic idea about what we can do to benefit others. If fully enlightened beings are limited in this way, how much more limited are we at this stage? We have to come to terms with the fact that we can't immediately help others to the degree and in the way we would like. On the other hand, there is a lot we can do, even when our tsewa is still impeded and our heart is not nearly as open as it will be one day.

Just in itself, expanding our own tender heart brings benefit to others. By cultivating impartial, free-flowing warmth, we automatically orient ourselves to be in favor of anything that enhances the well-being of others and against anything that causes them suffering. The heart of tsewa naturally and continually expresses wishes on others' behalf. We can't see, in any obvious way, how and when these wishes actually benefit other beings, especially those who are far away. Nonetheless, our wishes do support them, especially when we wish for them to experience tsewa in their own lives, to be able to express their own warm heart and to receive that tenderness from others.

When we think about beings who are undergoing great suffering, it is natural to feel helpless. For example, what can we do for a refugee family that has just crossed the Mediterranean on an overcrowded rubber boat and is now facing a precarious future? We could wish for these people, who have lost everything and gone through such a dangerous ordeal, to meet kind people, to find a nice home, and so on. These are certainly good wishes to make, but whether they come true will also be based on many other factors that will take a long time to play out. On the other hand, we can simply open our heart to them and wish for them to have an abundance of love and warmth in their lives and in their minds. We can further wish that this love gives them the resilience to overcome their challenges—the strength, ability, and resourcefulness to do what is necessary to live well.

I believe that this kind of wish has an immediate effect. It is similar to when you tell someone, "I'm thinking about you." When you're going through a difficult time, knowing that someone is thinking about you touches you and gives you strength. It makes you feel supported. Of course, in the case of the refugees, they're not aware of our well-wishes. Even so, when we express love to people who are beyond the reach of our communication, there is some transmission of the energy of our tsewa. They do receive it, and it does make a difference. When we send tsewa to any beings in this world, near or far, human or nonhuman, our warm, purely positive energy touches them. It gives them more resilience to make it through whatever they have to endure and to overcome their karma sooner rather than later. When we make such a connection to other beings, they are no longer alone, no longer lost somewhere in the abyss of samsara, untouched by love.

We have the ability to send others positive energy because we have accumulated a store of positive karma in our mindstream. Whenever we do anything on behalf of others, we sow a seed of positive karma that remains latent in our consciousness until the right conditions appear for it to ripen. First, the effect appears in our mind, and then it shows up in our external world. For example, when we act generously, we develop an internal feeling of wealth that is then reflected in our external world as increased abundance. In Buddhist terminology, this positive karma is known as "merit." We accumulate merit whenever our physical deeds, our speech, or our thoughts are oriented to the welfare of others. In other words, we accumulate merit when our body, speech, and mind are in sync with tsewa.

If we use the merit we have accumulated to satisfy the self that we cling to out of delusion, our store will rapidly diminish, and our heart will become tighter and tighter. This is because focusing on the singular, isolated self is the antithesis of tsewa. The positive actions we have done in the past will continue to bear their fruit, but if we don't continue to keep our heart open to others, we will only accumulate negativity. Our precious merit will be wasted on pleasant experiences that are fleeting and ultimately meaningless.

Therefore, the best thing we can do with our merit is to offer it freely for the benefit of others. Whenever you do anything meritorious, no matter how small, you can make a conscious wish that the positive energy from your action will have a vast effect, like an acorn growing into a giant oak tree. This is not a farfetched idea when we contemplate the interconnected nature of all things. Everything we do or even think has endless, rippling repercussions. For this reason, we don't have to feel helpless about benefiting others. We always have something to give.

By sending your merit to others, you are not losing anything yourself. On the contrary, the more merit you offer to others, the more your heart opens; the more your heart opens, the more positive your actions become; the more positive your actions become, the more merit you accumulate and are able to offer. If we know how to work with merit, it becomes an infinitely self-replenishing fuel that will eventually take us and others all the way to enlightenment.

When we dedicate our merit to others, however, we need to believe that it actually reaches them. This requires faith because we can't literally see the results of our wishes. We don't know how or when the effects take place. It is said that only the buddhas can see the vast workings of cause and effect. We who have a more limited view of karma can only trust that our merit is helping others, without knowing all the specifics.

Having such trust is a much more positive attitude than thinking we can't be making a difference for others unless we can see how cause and effect are operating on a physical level. That is an extremely limited vision of what we can do. Closing down to that kind of limitation is also philosophically narrow-minded, for how is it essentially different from thinking that nothing in the world exists beyond what we can see with our own eyes?

We are often skeptical about the power of thought. This is strange because we are always struggling with our own thoughts. Most of us are more scared of our own mind than of anything else. We're scared of our anger, our reactions, our confusion. To be scared of them, we have to believe that they are powerful. Yet at the same time, we can be so skeptical about the power of our good wishes and compassionate thoughts on behalf of others. Even if miracles happen as a result of our prayers, we can keep insisting on our skepticism, finding other explanations. This is how we tend to undermine our strength and get caught up in low self-esteem.

Your body is limited in where it can go and be. You may spend all day within the walls of your workplace and all night within the walls of your house. And within those walls, there are few other sentient beings. But your mind and heart have no boundaries. Our connections with others are not limited by walls. Nor are our responsibilities limited to those we see in our daily lives. It is true that we may have more immediate responsibilities to our families and those who directly depend on us, but if our bigger vision is bodhichitta, the wish to attain enlightenment for the benefit of all beings, then our responsibility is to all beings. While taking care of those who are close to us, we need to open our heart further to those outside of this small circle. In this life, we have a close karmic connection to some beings, while the overwhelming majority we never see or have any contact with. But if we keep in mind that all beings are identical in wanting to be happy and free from suffering, we can diminish our habitual distinction between near and far. In this way, we can keep strengthening and expanding our feeling of being connected to everyone suffering in samsara, until our longing to benefit others becomes so powerful that it overshadows all our self-centered or narrow-minded wishes.

As your heart opens and your actions become more and more oriented to the benefit of others, you will accumulate tremendous merit that you can harness for the purpose of benefiting individuals, groups of beings, and eventually all sentient beings. You should also dedicate your merit for your own enlightenment, so that you may swiftly become the perfect guide to help others realize their innate, selfless, tender heart. By directing your positive karma in these ways, you will automatically create connections and situations in which you will be able to benefit others in the future—if not in this life, then in future lives. You will lay the groundwork for being able to bring all beings, one by one, to the full realization of their enlightened nature. This is the magnificent fruit of tsewa.

8

TSEWA AND RELATIONSHIPS:
THE NEED FOR DISCERNMENT

Tenderness and warmth are what enable sentient beings to have positive relationships with each other. For example, when we express warmth to animals, they feel touched and at ease. Naturally, they begin to open up and express the same kind of warmth to us. Because they understand that we are on their side, that we want the best for them, they are able to form a bond of mutual trust and closeness with us.

This can even happen with animals that are predators by nature, such as tigers or lions. There is the well-known story about the two men who bought a lion cub from Harrods, the department store in London. They named the cub Christian and raised him in their home. When Christian grew too big, they released him into the wild in Kenya, where he started his own family. Years later, the two men visited Christian, who had grown to be enormous. He ran toward them, knocked them over, and hugged them as he used to, with his paws on their shoulders.

Even a fish that you can buy at a pet store is capable of responding to your tender heart. Human beings and fish couldn't appear more different from each other. Fish come in so many bright colors. They have to be underwater to breathe. Their sense perceptions are so different from ours that it's as if they experience a completely different world. From our point of view, it's hard to tell that they have any intelligence at all. And if there are several fish of the same species in the tank, we can barely tell them apart.

When you first start to interact with a fish, it tends to swim away. However, after a short while, if you keep your tender heart open to it, it recognizes that you're not a threat. But that is not all—it also knows that you are different from the rocks and plants in its tank. It understands that you are in favor of its well-being, whereas the rocks and plants are neutral. This ability to distinguish an inanimate object from a sentient being who cares for it shows that the fish can make meaning from the experiences of its senses. Thus, even tiny fish are able to develop a sense of closeness with us, a feeling of sharing a world and a life together.

If we can give tsewa to and receive it from animals, whose minds, perceptions, and experiences are so different from ours, then how much more natural tenderness can we exchange with human beings? We have a great deal more potential for mutual understanding and common experience.

On the other hand, in relationships with human beings, there are many ways we can go wrong, and many tricky situations we can get into, especially with those who are closest to us. Even if we value loving relationships above everything else in life, we are still subject to the various impediments previously discussed, such as resentment, suspicion, biases, and expectations. It is so easy to be confused when these issues come up, so easy to let our mental and emotional turmoil overshadow the simple and natural expression of our warm heart.

In some sense, it comes down to protecting our heart from our head. This head of ours continually comes up with confused ideas and stories that feed our self-centered emotions and cause our heart to contract. We believe this egocentric side of our conceptual mind a little too much. We trust that it has an accurate read on situations. We give it credit for being able to fathom the depths of others' minds and hearts. But why do we think this small-mindedness deserves such credit? Have our tsewa-impeding thoughts about others ever enhanced our relationships in any way? Or have they only contracted our heart and, in so doing, shrunk our whole world? We would like somehow to mold relationships and people according to our preferences. Despite our history of never succeeding in this area, we tend to keep trying this approach again and again. And even if we could somehow make others behave in the way we wanted, would that bring us lasting happiness and joy? How would that be possible without tsewa at the center of our relationships?

Instead of relying on our neurotic thoughts and preferences to guide us, we must strive to cultivate unconditional tsewa. If we can move toward keeping our heart open at all times, we will find that our relationships naturally keep getting better. Whatever karmic history we have with other people, instead of continuing to struggle so much with the outer situation, we can always improve things by placing our reliance in tsewa.

But does this mean that there is no place in our relationships for conceptual mind? Is it best to shut off our thinking and simply let the heart set its own course? No, that is not the way of the bodhisattvas. It is important to clarify this point. Keeping our heart open at all times does not mean surrendering the positive aspects of our conceptual mind—our critical intelligence and discernment. Tsewa and critical intelligence are not in opposition. On the contrary, as we develop wisdom and skillful means, we can use these faculties to complement our tender heart and to make our altruistic actions more effective.

If we shut off our intelligence and blindly go through life relying on our naïve idea of a loving heart, we will make a lot of mistakes. One of the most likely outcomes is that we will turn into a doormat. Many of the people we would like to help may start to take advantage of us, whether consciously or unconsciously. So at the outset of this path, it is important to emphasize that a bodhisattva is not a doormat. While keeping unconditionally positive feelings toward other beings in their hearts, bodhisattvas have boundaries. We must also have boundaries, if we aspire to bring true benefit to others—whether in our day-to-day life, or ultimately as a perfect guide leading other beings to enlightenment.

Once a Brahmin girl asked the Buddha to marry her. He had to say no, even though it caused her pain. When his jealous cousin Devadatta asked the Buddha to make him his regent, the Buddha had to say no. If he had said yes to either of these people because of some misplaced idea of "unconditional love," what would the Dharma have become? How much would humanity have lost? The wiser a person is, the better he or she knows how to relate with others appropriately in all situations. A true sage has mastered the art of keeping the heart open while being guided by the discerning mind.

If we behave naïvely with others, we will neither help them nor help our own spiritual progress. The Buddhist teachings generally emphasize the motivation behind actions. It is said that whether an act is positive or negative depends on whether the motivation behind it is altruistic or self-centered. However, this is not an authorization for us to act blindly, as if hiding behind our simplistic "good" intentions. The Dharma does not defy common sense. Motivation is indeed crucial, but we also need to look ahead—to the best of our ability—to the results of our actions. From there, we can rely on both tsewa and critical intelligence to determine which course to take.

In raising children, for example, we will not be successful if we trust too blindly in our parental affection. If we overindulge children, they will become spoiled. They will grow up with a sense of entitlement that will cause them to step on others to advance their own aims. If we set boundaries, they are much more likely to grow up to be decent people who are able to open their hearts to others. Children don't set their own boundaries. Their parents and teachers have to do that for them. So the way to behave in accord with genuine tsewa is to look ahead to the likely results, which should not be so mysterious—they have been demonstrated over and over again through all the ages of human history.

There are some differences, of course, in how we should behave with adults. Yet most adults have a similar tendency to act spoiled when they sense that we have no boundaries. Overindulging people of any age makes it impossible to have a good relationship. This happens often between spouses or partners and between good friends. We think we are bending over backward for someone because of our deep care. We love and we love more, we give and we give more—and in the end, instead of appreciating us, they may very well end up resenting us. We thought we were doing them a great kindness, but instead we were hindering their ability to stand on their own two feet.

Setting boundaries can bring up a lot of conflict in our mind. If someone is invading our space, being demanding, or clinging to us out of insecurity, we know this is not helpful for either of us. Still we may have qualms about setting boundaries. "Is this too harsh, too uncaring, too uncompassionate? I want to be kind and compassionate, not any of those negative things." With our children, the fears are usually worse. We may think, "Will my child grow up to hate me? Will my child be psychologically damaged?" This kind of confusion makes us weak and unable to act in a way that benefits anyone.

When our head starts to spin with so many thoughts of self-doubt, that is a sign that our heart is closing down. We have given ourselves over to the neurotic, self-centered side of our conceptual mind. Our thinking, which appears to be focused on someone else, is actually oriented toward self-protection. "How will this affect *me*? What will it say about *me*? How will it make *me* look?"

This is another place where wisdom and discernment can save the day. When we are in the throes of this kind of insecurity and confusion, if we examine the condition of our heart, we will see that it is not actually open to others. It is not warm with the glow of tsewa. When we are in that state, especially in relation to those who are closest to us, it is easy to feel stuck. It is easy to feel weak. What can we do to regain our strength?

Here it is helpful to distinguish between the open, unconditional tenderness of tsewa and the sticky feeling of enmeshment that tends to come up in close relationships. We feel enmeshed when we see others as extensions of ourselves. If you see your spouse, for example, as an extension of yourself, you may feel that you have a claim on your spouse, or that your spouse has a claim on you. This can lead to frequent power struggles. Sometimes you feel entitled to be bossy; other times you feel you are treated like a slave. Your life together could turn into a series of negotiations and compromises—more like a business transaction or a chess game than a loving relationship. Because of your insecurity in relation to the other person, you may find yourself continually seeking ways, from blatant to passive-aggressive, of gaining control.

But none of these methods actually leads to a feeling of security. Instead of feeling love in the relationship, you may feel fear. Instead of treating each other with respect, you may end up treating each other as means to fulfill your wishes. Instead of helping each other grow, you may hinder each other's progress. Both of you may feel more and more codependent—and more and more uncertain about who you really are as individuals.

It is natural, and almost inevitable, for our closest relationships to have some taint of this enmeshment. Since we all have the habit of clinging to a self, we can't help seeing other people, at least to some extent, as instruments of our self-cherishing and self-protecting. Even a mother—the universal symbol of unconditional love—is not free from self-attachment in relation to her child. If her self weren't involved, why would she feel so much more worry and anxiety for her own children than for anyone else's? It is important to acknowledge this tendency we all share if our aim is to refine and expand our tsewa so we can benefit wider and wider circles of sentient beings.

It is said that there is a certain kind of swan that can separate milk from water when they are mixed together. We must learn to be like that swan and separate tsewa, which always brings joy and strength to us and others, from all the biological and self-oriented factors that can turn love into confusion. You can train yourself to see your close relationships in a different way—a healthier way—that will bring about more tenderness and less tension. This is by seeing the other person, not as an extension of yourself, but as an individual of her own—a fellow sentient being who wishes to be happy and free from suffering. Your spouse, your child, your parent, your friend, your teacher, your student—whoever it is—is just another sentient being with her own mind; her own past, present, and future; her own need to give and receive warmth. For this relatively short span of time, karma has brought you together. But this does not give you a claim on one another. Rather, it gives you a wonderful opportunity to enjoy mutual love and caring. It gives you a chance to water your seed of tsewa. This is the best way we can share our time together. This is what makes our eyes sparkle and our hearts fill with bliss.

There are some relationships, however, that are not workable—at least not in this lifetime. The karmic causes and conditions are simply not in favor of the relationship. The best solution is to move on. This is not a failure; it is simply a manifestation of karma from the past. We don't have absolute control over how past karma manifests. But we can control how we sow the karmic seeds that will determine our future. We have a choice about what happens next, what happens in our heart.

When a relationship ends, it is common for one or both parties to be resentful. Sometimes the pain can be so great that we become bitter about love and tenderness in general. It seems easier and more peaceful to keep our heart closed. It is crucial not to cave in to this self-destructive way of reacting. We have to think about the downfalls of holding on to a grudge and cutting ourselves off from tsewa. We have to contemplate the benefits of keeping our heart open to all beings and bravely striding forward along the bodhisattva path. And then we have to apply the appropriate remedies to our grudge.

When we move on, we may also feel haunted by doubts that we have done the right thing, that we have acted as the kind, compassionate person we would like to be. This can be a more intense version of the qualms we feel when setting boundaries. But sometimes moving on *is* the most compassionate thing we can do, even if it causes temporary pain. If we always maintain a feeling of tenderness toward the other person, and if we apply our conceptual mind intelligently, not neurotically, we can trust that our actions will be beneficial, however they may appear at first glance. Then, when the other person is no longer in our physical presence, we can still make aspirations to benefit him when circumstances change. We can make prayers on his behalf and dedicate our merit for him to have joy and tsewa in his life.

In our minds, we tend to confine each of our relationships to this single lifetime. When we lose people, we think they are gone from us forever. But considered from the view of countless lifetimes, we are continually meeting and parting from each other. At this particular moment, only an infinitesimal fraction of beings are within the reach of our direct benefit. But if our main purpose in life is to open our heart wider and wider, then every time we meet with and part from another sentient being, we are making a meaningful connection for the future. Even if we have a negative encounter or a relationship that ends badly, our bodhichitta intention and the continual tenderness of our heart will ensure that one day we will come back together in a more positive relationship. From there, we will be in a better position to help ourselves and the other person come out of the confusion of samsara. And once we have reached our ultimate goal of enlightenment, it will just be a matter of time before we're able to connect to all beings and profoundly benefit them all, whether they are temporarily near or far.

9

MEETING DEATH
WITH AN OPEN HEART

In the course of our lives, we experience loss after loss. There is no way to count how many things we have lost so far and how many we will lose in the future. Sometimes loss is what we want. For example, when we cut our hair and nails, we lose them on purpose. In other cases, loss doesn't bother us because we see it as just an ordinary part of life. Days go by, seasons change, the world changes—and for the most part, we let it happen without painfully trying to hold on.

Then there are the losses that torment us: loss of good fortune, loss of physical and mental abilities, loss of loved ones, loss of our own precious life. We can feel agony because of our strong attachment to these things. We tend to want to keep them forever, but that is impossible, no matter how attached we are.

For the majority, the most devastating loss of all is the loss of this life. At that time, we are likely, first of all, to suffer from physical weakness, discomfort, and pain. On top of that, there is the tremendous fear and anxiety of having to leave behind this world and everything familiar to us to face something completely unknown. The final phase of life is the time when all our attachments tend to rise up and bring us greater suffering than ever before.

I have been with many people at the end of their lives. It is a difficult time for almost everyone, but I have seen some people do very well. They have shown great resilience and suffered little from fear, anxiety, depression, regret, and grief. Often they have gone through physical discomfort, but even that is lessened. They have deeply appreciated their life's journey, all the events in it, the ups and downs, and all the people they have known and encountered. Some have even met death in a state of complete joy and fearlessness.

What do these people have in common? What have they relied on in their final hours? And what can we rely on when we are in that position, which will happen sooner than we know? It is not the knowledge and skills we have acquired for successfully negotiating this life. It is not how famous we are or how many people want to surround our bed. It is not the expensive medical treatments and hospital equipment that our big savings account has made possible. It is not even the religious doctrines that we have followed and believed in.

From what I have observed, psychological and emotional well-being at the end of life depends on two qualities: a tender heart with tsewa flowing abundantly to others, and a positive attitude. When I have seen people with these two qualities, I have witnessed their resilience as well. They have faced the difficulties of dying and death with ease. These people have inspired me, and I am determined to cultivate these qualities myself.

When the heart is completely open, there is no longer any room for small, shortsighted attachment to the self. Our tendency to self-inflict pain by cherishing and protecting the ego has nowhere left to hang out. When our heart is full of warm feelings toward others, we are connected to the source of all goodness in the world. We are in touch with the only reliable source of happiness and peace. In this state, whatever happens to our body—even its final destruction—cannot take us down to the depths of misery. This is how tsewa becomes our greatest refuge from the sufferings of old age, sickness, and death.

To go along with a tender heart, we also need to have a habit of positive thinking. This does not mean being naïvely or superficially "positive." It does not mean engaging in wishful thinking or propping ourselves up with affirmations that we don't believe. Genuine positive thinking means making the best of whatever happens in our lives. It is a way of using circumstances that are normally considered negative to bring us along the spiritual path. Committing to a positive outlook forces us to be creative and think outside the box. Instead of reacting predictably to the troubles that come up in our lives, we use our intelligence to come up with different approaches.

We can use our suffering in many ways: to wake ourselves up to what other beings are going through, to increase our love and compassion, and to strengthen the resolve of our bodhichitta—our aspiration to attain enlightenment in order to relieve all the suffering of samsara. When we are able to make the most of our suffering in these ways, we can feel grateful for it. We can see our suffering—even the suffering of dying—as a great blessing in our life. What could be a more positive attitude than this?

Another part of having a positive attitude is putting things in perspective. We all feel that our lives are very precious. How could there be a bigger loss than the loss of this life? But if we see this transition as loss and loss only, that will only intensify our clinging, to the point where it will make us feel devastated. Furthermore, this is a nihilistic view. It is not how someone who truly understands cause and effect sees things.

Yes, death is a loss, but it is also a gain. The end of a life is like the end of a year or the end of a day. Today has been a great day, precious and productive. But tomorrow may well be a better day. As we keep opening our heart further and further, we accumulate merit and attract good conditions for our well-being and growth. In our next life, we are likely to find ourselves with even more supportive circumstances for continuing to develop our tsewa. For someone who has embarked on the bodhisattva path, another life is another chance to make progress. It is something to look forward to rather than something to fear. At the end of this life, we do have to part from our loved ones, but this is also not a final loss. From the Buddhist teachings' point of view, in past lives, we have all been each other's parents and children, sisters and brothers, lovers and friends. We have all met many times in the past and will continue to meet in the future, until we are all free from the suffering of samsara. Death is not a final parting.

Even with this view, for most of us, there may still be some anxiety about the dissolution of this body and the unknown future. But it is possible to develop a totally carefree attitude about death, like Patrul Rinpoche, one of the great masters from the lineage of teachers before me. A practitioner like him, whose mind is governed only by bodhichitta, is equally happy with a long or short life. Which is better depends on which will more rapidly fulfill one's ultimate aspiration to attain enlightenment. At the end of a life like that, there is no sense of holding on and no fear of what is to come.

The beauty of having a human brain is that you can imagine the future and plan for it. You can imagine and compare different scenarios and choose which one you would like to aim for. At the time of death, there are two main scenarios to consider: either you die with a warm heart and a positive attitude, or you die with a cold heart and a negative attitude. This choice is up to you, but you have to make the choice as soon as possible. If you wait until you're on your deathbed to open your heart and become a positive thinker, you will discover that it is too late. We can't trade our bad habits for good habits at the drop of a hat. It takes a long time to get over bad habits and adopt good ones. While we are relatively young and healthy, we need to use as much of our time as possible to create favorable conditions for our death and our transition to the next life.

Having this aim will not only help us in our last moments; it will help us every day of our lives. Sometimes we see elderly people who, despite the limited time they have left, are incredibly fearless and passionate about their lives. Their spunky quality is so inspiring to me. What accounts for this spunkiness? These people are often very ordinary and are not necessarily practitioners of any established religion. But what they all have is the exuberance of a warm heart and the radiance of positive thinking. They have discovered the formula both for living life with the maximum enjoyment and meaning and for departing from life with the maximum peace and confidence. This is my greatest wish for all of us.

10

THE WORLD AND THE FUTURE

We are at a critical juncture in world history. The elements of our environment are going through a rapid process of change that threatens the future of our planet. Relations among countries have reached dangerous levels of disharmony. We are seeing widespread violence based on race, religion, and social and economic inequality. The well-being of this world and everyone living in it is in jeopardy. How we respond at this time will make an immense difference to the prospect of happiness for countless sentient beings. The stakes couldn't be higher.

There are so many ways we can try to benefit the world and the beings in it. We can become doctors, nurses, activists, teachers, scientists, organizers, diplomats, writers, artists, political leaders, religious leaders, community leaders, Peace Corps volunteers, environmentalists, philanthropists. We can simply be good people who behave thoughtfully and altruistically to the people and animals around us. We can even spend most of our time alone, engaged in spiritual practice. There is no one particular role that anyone must play to respond well to our current situation.

But whatever you do, if it is to be truly beneficial to the world, it must begin with your tender heart. No positive action is separate from tsewa. All the imbalance and disharmony we are seeing has come from the opposite of tsewa—a closed heart and a self-centered mind. If your intention is to promote balance and harmony—among human beings; with animals; with trees, rivers, mountains, and the Earth itself—you must put tsewa at the center. You must make opening your heart your highest priority in life. From there, all positive outer results will naturally follow, as flowers naturally arise in the springtime.

Any community, movement, or educational endeavor—if it is to have any value—must be founded on tenderness. It must be based on the principle that all sentient beings want to be happy and free from suffering, and that the happiness and suffering of others is as important as our own. Without tsewa, every religion, every spiritual group, every attempt to reform government or address injustice or overcome terrorism or resolve conflicts will be meaningless. And if these groups and endeavors have anti-tsewa elements, such as if they are one-sided or full of deep-seated motives to promote certain groups at the expense of others, they will only add to the negativity and suffering of the world.

Our future will depend on how much we put our trust in the goodness and effectiveness of tsewa. It will depend on how much we make the most of our innate tenderness and how much we foster that tenderness in others. It will depend on how much we honor tsewa for what it is: the source of all well-being, the ultimate wish-fulfilling jewel.

Tsewa is the only thing that can give us the strength and resilience to overcome the challenges that the world presents. Even though we all have this tender heart, there are always certain individuals, who because of their intense confusion and their ability to influence people, spread pain and chaos to many others. But when people develop the strength of tsewa, they act as buffers to protect others from such harm and influence. When many people collectively put their trust in the good heart, it is like erecting a wall that prevents the fire of confusion from spreading.

Seen in this light, opening the heart is much more than just a spiritual practice. It is a way we can all enhance our relations with the world and with each other. It has social, economic, political, and environmental benefits. It is a way of navigating the world. It is a survival skill.

What the world needs most is education in tsewa. We need more people to learn how to look into their own hearts and see the vast difference in their well-being when their hearts are open and when they are closed. We need more people to see for themselves how tsewa is the source of all happiness and goodness in the world. In particular, people in positions of power, influence, or responsibility—such as people in government, the military, and law enforcement—need to fill their hearts with tenderness. Otherwise, they will likely enact their duties based on a hunger for power, blind ideology, fear, or some other self-serving agenda.

Therefore, my request to you is that you not only cultivate your own tenderness of heart, but that you promote tsewa in the world. Please educate your children, your students, and others about tsewa in whatever way, with whatever words, and to whatever degree you think it will be most effective. This is not an encouragement to spread Buddhist ideas. It is an encouragement to help people make the most of their own birthright, their most precious inheritance.

The people of this modern world are interconnected and intermingled like never before. In this way, modern society enjoys an unprecedented richness. In the past, there were not many places where you could be among people whose ancestors came from Europe, Asia, Africa, and America; who were male, female, transgender, gay, and straight; who grew up with so many different religious and nonreligious ideas and beliefs. The world was much more segregated. But now such diversity and mixture are common.

Some people find such diversity to be threatening. There will always be those who want to go back to how things were before. Some may even think that turning back the tide would actually reduce conflict. But there is no way to go back in time. Any attempts to impose a more segregated society will damage that society severely. On the other hand, this is not about ignoring the differences among people, the details that make every person unique. We are not talking about becoming "color blind" and failing to notice what is in front of us. Variety is part of what makes our world so rich. It is something to honor rather than a problem to solve.

The only way forward is for people to bind themselves closer together than ever before. The glue that will bind us has to be our common tenderness of heart. If we learn how to cultivate tsewa, we can see each other as members of a large, wonderful extended family. With that view, our diversity will only be an advantage, an aid to our individual and collective growth. It will give us more to embrace, more occasions for opening our hearts.

But is this vision of tsewa spreading throughout the world just a fantasy? To me, it is not. In fact, it is already underway. There are so many noble people doing noble things in the world. Look at what Doctors Without Borders is doing. Look at the Red Cross nurses, the social workers, the journalists, the teachers. Look at the movements taking place across the globe on behalf of peace, the environment, gender equality, social justice, conscious living, and animal rights. There has never been a time when so many people have joined together to make positive things happen all over the world. The world is full of good citizens, and that includes you. Look at yourself and all the good things you are doing to help others, to open your heart, to follow your innate desire to make a difference in the world. What you are doing already, despite your current limitations, is beautiful. You must acknowledge all of this and let yourself be touched by the goodness that surrounds you.

The majority of people aspire to contribute to the world and to each others' lives. The majority understand that the greatest joy and meaning in our lives comes from what we give to others, not what we take. Most of us also understand that going against someone else's welfare will undermine our own welfare. This kind of logic makes sense to people. That is why it will prevail over confusion and ignorance.

From this point of view, we are not living in a dark age. We are living in the dawn of light. Even though there could be more goodness and altruism, even though greed, injustice, and aggression cause tremendous suffering every day, we must take some time to reflect on what is going right. Those who inflict pain on others out of their confusion and ignorance are a small minority of this world's seven billion plus people. If we lose perspective and overestimate their prevalence, then our inspiration will be hijacked by skepticism and negative thinking. There are those—especially in extreme religious groups and some portions of the media and politics—who attempt to serve their own agendas by promoting negative, polarizing thinking. There are others who have no agenda but are habitually negative. But if our aim is to open our heart and let its natural, exuberant warmth spread to others, we must not let this kind of thinking infiltrate our mind.

The more open our heart is, the more we feel others' suffering as our own. But that doesn't mean we feel depressed and despondent. The suffering of others doesn't weigh us down because we are buoyed by the warmth of our tenderness toward them. For someone who is guided by bodhichitta, the wish to benefit all beings by attaining enlightenment, living in samsara is a joyful experience. Every minute that your heart is open is a minute to cherish. There is no sense of heaviness and no bewilderment about what you should be doing. Every moment, there is something you can do to benefit sentient beings. Even if you are alone, you can warm your heart toward others, you can make aspirations and prayers on their behalf, and you can dedicate your merit to their well-being and their eventual enlightenment. The ability to perform altruistic activities throughout the day—day in and day out, year after year, life after life—is what keeps the bodhisattva feeling so light. It is what brings the perpetual smile to the face of His Holiness the Dalai Lama and others like him.

The future of the world depends on tsewa. This is fortunate because tsewa is something we are all born with. We all have a heart that can open, and we can feel the difference between an open heart and a closed heart. Out of habit or ignorance, we may choose to keep our heart closed, or we may not realize we have a choice. But when we begin to understand the power of tsewa and how we can cultivate it, our innate wisdom will guide us toward greater and greater warmth and tenderness, until there is no difference between our heart and the heart of the Buddha, the perfect compassionate guide. We all have this infinite potential, and we will realize it sooner rather than later. Thanks to tsewa—the wish-fulfilling jewel that you and I and all sentient beings possess—the future is in good hands.